UNDERSTANDING
EMOTIONAL
INTELLIGENCE
in

90
Minutes

Jan Childs

First published in 2007 by Management Books 2000 Ltd
Forge House, Limes Road, Kemble, Cirencester
Gloucestershire, GL7 6AD, UK
Tel: 0044 (0) 1285 771441
Fax: 0044 (0) 1285 771055
E-mail: info@mb2000.com
Web: www.mb2000.com

Printed and bound in Great Britain by 4edge Ltd of Hockley, Essex – www.4edge.co.uk

British Library Cataloguing in Publication Data is available
ISBN 9781852525255

*Dedicated to the advancement of ethical emotional intelligence and
the promotion of personal wellbeing
&
In loving memory of my father*

*For the generations to come, and especially for
Tom & Sophie*

About the Author

Jan Childs is driven by a passionate belief in the value of emotional intelligence to both our business and personal lives, and committed to the advancement of effective leadership and teamwork, and the promotion of personal wellbeing. As a specialist in EQ consultancy, strategic leadership, team development and executive coaching, an author of numerous papers on emotional intelligence and the co-author of *Mindchange – The Power of Emotionally Intelligent Leadership* (Management Books 2000), Jan draws on a range and depth of experience that she continues to learn from and build on. Her work with clients ranges from executive leadership and team coaching, advising on company policies and practices that put emotional intelligence at the forefront of corporate strategy, to working with teams and individuals at the front line in service provision.

Contents

Contents

Introduction

> *'What is a human being but a bundle of emotional nerves?'*
>
> Tahseen Hassan
> (The husband of Margaret Hassan – following her abduction and subsequent murder in Baghdad, October 2004)

And as my friend Karen so astutely commented when we were discussing the difficulties of trying to understand and deal with perplexing human behaviour (including our own!) and the merits of emotional intelligence: *'Aren't we all complex simmering cauldrons of emotions when we look underneath?'*

Interest in emotional intelligence and how we can develop it to enrich and improve our lives has been growing exponentially since Daniel Goleman's book, *Emotional Intelligence,* was published in 1995. And the once traditional measure of intelligence based on intellectual ability (IQ) is now generally accepted as being too narrowly focused to judge the human mental capacity needed to manage our lives in a world of accelerating change and complexity. As Einstein put it so succinctly: *'We should take care not to make intellect our god. It has of course powerful muscles, but no personality'.*

So, why is there such a high level of interest in emotional intelligence, and is it any different from what may have been previously referred to as maturity, common sense or wisdom? And most importantly, how can we develop it?

Emotional intelligence, or *'emotional quotient'* (EQ) as it's often referred to, is about putting recognition and understanding of emotions to the forefront of our thinking rather than maintaining a focus on, or preference for, intellectual reasoning. But because it's about emotions, and dealing with these with an increased awareness and understanding of their impact, it can be challenging to put into practice – especially for those who prefer to keep the traditional *'stiff upper lip'* approach. It could also be argued that those who purport either not to understand emotional intelligence or choose to dismiss its relevance to the wider debate on human intelligence may do so because of the personal implications of the need for changed behaviour.

The establishment of the term *'emotional intelligence'* reflects its recognition as a legitimate topic for intellectual dialogue and a more open acceptance of the value of questioning how effectively we deal with both our own and others' emotions. For a greater number of people and in a wider range of contexts it has unleashed an enhanced awareness of the importance of human emotions and their impact on our lives.

While emotional intelligence brings a heightened acknowledgement of the impact of emotions to both our working and personal lives it's categorically not a *'pink and fluffy'* approach – as evidenced by increasing recognition of its value by senior leaders in the military as well as in business and commerce. Interest in EQ development is driven not only by seeking increased personal wellbeing and more rewarding relationships, but also in addressing the continuing productivity challenge of achieving *'more with less'* through improved individual, team and organisational performance.

Since Daniel Goleman first popularised the term there have been extensive discussions and numerous publications about what emotional intelligence means and how both to measure it and to achieve it, and there has been much debate concerning the extent to which its meaning has been misinterpreted or embellished. The aim of this book, in 90 minutes reading time, is to provide a broad understanding of emotional intelligence and its application, rather than to get into an in-depth intellectual argument about semantics.

'Understanding Emotional Intelligence in 90 minutes' provides an overview of the background to emotional intelligence as a concept,

outlines its benefits, and includes best and worst practice illustrations to highlight emotional intelligence (or its absence!) in practice. Lessons are noted from business, politics, the public sector and society in general. Its primary focus and most important emphasis is however the 'how to' – that is, how we can learn to be more emotionally intelligent in both our work and private lives. What is emphasised throughout is the foundation of self-awareness and reflective practice needed on the personal journey towards developing a higher level of emotional competence.

Throughout the book, a number of quotes are highlighted relating to the associated section as well as to emotional intelligence in general. I hope you find these as thought-provoking, inspiring and memorable as I do. EQ Learning Resources including books, articles, exercises and poetry, plus more quotes, can be found on www.eq4u.co.uk.

1

Opening Reflections

Three things to establish about emotional intelligence

So, what's it all about?

As a foundation for understanding what emotional intelligence is all about, and before looking at its exponents, definitions, benefits and the *'how to'*, there are three key things to establish.

The first is that although the term *'emotional intelligence'* may only have been in use in recent years it is clearly nothing new, but has been an essential element in shaping our ability to interact with each other since human beings first communicated.

Despite Daniel Goleman's profile at the forefront of published material on emotional intelligence, the first definition of the term *'emotional intelligence'* is generally credited to John Mayer, (University of New Hampshire), and Peter Salovey (Yale) in the 1980s in their published studies on the interaction between emotion and cognition. An American psychologist Edward Lee Thorndike, in referring to the behaviour traits now seen as being emotionally intelligent, did however use the term *'social intelligence'* some sixty years previously, when in 1920 he described the skill of interacting effectively with other people – the essence of being emotionally intelligent.

Interestingly, Professor Nicholas Humphrey, a British psychologist also coined the term *'Machiavellian intelligence'*, loosely described as *'the capacity for successful political engagement with social groups'*, which could also be interpreted as being *'emotionally intelligent'*. His 1975 essay *'The Social Function of Intellect'* suggested a need for *'social skills'* analysis as a test of what he described as *'high level intelligence'*. His paper put forward the theory that human beings have evolved to be *'natural psychologists'* who use models of their own minds as a basis for understanding others – an essential attribute of emotional intelligence!

Also in 1975, Howard Gardner formulated the concept of *'multiple intelligences'*, including both *'interpersonal'* and *'intrapersonal'* intelligences, both firmly associated with the concept of emotional intelligence. What Gardner additionally argued was that a person's intelligence varies according to *'how you are smart'*, and not *'how smart you are'*.

So, emotional intelligence is definitely not new – and intelligence quotient (IQ) is not the only measure of human intelligence.

The second thing to establish is that emotional intelligence applies to everyone at every stage and in all walks of life.

Building effective relationships is something we need to do if we are to be successful in the numerous and varied roles that we have in our lives. Parents communicating with their children, teachers trying to engage the attention of their pupils, colleagues interacting with each other at work, friends engaged in social activities, doctors and nurses dealing with their patients, and anyone in a situation providing customer service are just a few examples. While this book is aimed primarily at leaders and managers, the concept applies to everyone in every role, and to both our work and our personal lives.

Bringing an emotionally intelligent approach to how we deal with others can have significant pay-offs both personally and professionally, none more so than in the increasingly competitive and demanding corporate world. For, as Mark McCormack, the late Founder and Chairman of International Management Group (IMG) emphasised, *'Understanding human dynamics is still the most important thing in business.'*

> *'Emotional intelligence is a quick fix to achievement, but there's no quick fix to achieving it.'*
>
> Malaa Kapadia
> (Indian professor responsible for pioneering research into emotional intelligence)

The third – and most important – thing to establish is that the development and maintenance of emotional intelligence is a lifelong journey integrating self and other awareness with reflective management of behaviour in dealing with our own and others' emotions.

While human beings have an immense capacity to learn and develop, the well known expression *'you can't teach an old dog new tricks'* is often put forward as an argument for putting up barriers to learning for those who perceive themselves to have ingrained personality characteristics that they are either unwilling (*or convince themselves they are unable!*) to change. Potential for development of EQ, is however limited only by our attitude to learning. The willingness and ability to let go of established traits, and develop the mentality which encourages a continuous process of being open and ready to refine our approach and develop new ways of doing things is essential to effective learning. But because EQ relates to character and personality traits, rather than focusing on intellectual and technical abilities more closely associated with IQ, this approach to learning can be more problematic. And while a broad level of knowledge and understanding of what emotional intelligence is and how it can be developed may be gained in a relatively short time, achieving and maintaining emotional competence is likely to take considerably longer.

"The challenge in life is to die young as late as possible.'

Manfred Kets de Vries,
(Professor of Leadership, INSEAD Graduate
Business School)

My absolute favourite quote of all time!

2

Exponents, Definitions and Measurement

Key exponents of emotional intelligence

A web search for the term *'emotional intelligence'* currently brings up over 2 million entries, and numbers of books on the subject are now well into the hundreds. So, who are the key exponents of emotional intelligence and what does the term mean?

In addition to John Mayer and Peter Salovey, the number of people now involved in writing and presenting on emotional intelligence has grown significantly since the early days when Daniel Goleman first drew attention to the concept and advocated its benefits. Notable writers and exponents of emotional intelligence and its development include: Ayman Sawaf (co-author with Robert Cooper of *Executive EQ*), Annabel Jensen (pioneering educator teaching social-emotional skills and the author of four books on teaching and learning EQ), Pieter van Jaarsveld, (author of *Heart of a Winner: Developing your Emotional Intelligence*) Geetu Bharwaney (Author of *Emotionally Intelligent Living* and Founder of Ei World) Annie McKee (Co-Chair of the Teleos Leadership Institute, and co-author with Daniel Goleman and Richard Boyatzis of *Primal Leadership*), Malcolm Higgs and Vic Dulewicz (Henley Management College), Reuven Baron (co-editor of the *Handbook of Emotional Intelligence* and creator of the EQ-i® – and not forgetting the late Wayne Leon Payne, whose doctoral thesis entitled *'A study of emotion: Developing*

Emotional Intelligence' was published in 1985.

(My apologies to the individuals I may have missed by just highlighting those mentioned. There are now so many good people out there spreading the word about emotional intelligence that they are too numerous to mention – I'm inspired by and support them all.)

I was lucky enough to be at Peter Salovey's enlightening and engaging presentation on emotional intelligence at the Nexus EQ conference in Orlando, January 2004 (where he included an entertaining reference to former US President Bill Clinton's ability to emotionally engage with people!). For me, he was the most inspiring speaker at the conference, closely followed by Robert Cooper's moving and stimulating presentation, highlighting his experiences of childhood as influenced by his grandfather, and emphasising the danger of being 'a nodding dog on the windowsill of life'. If you ever get the opportunity to listen to either - they're both highly recommended!

Organisations set up to support and deliver learning and application of emotional intelligence include: Nexus EQ (USA), the *'Six Seconds'* EQ network, Emotional Intelligence Partnership, the Centre for Applied Emotional Intelligence and the Consortium for Research on Applied Emotional Intelligence in Organisations. Additionally, numerous consultancies now offer specialist EQ services, and emotional intelligence is also frequently cited as a key component of leadership development programmes.

What I find disturbing however, is that some of these consultancies in marketing their EQ specialism refer to emotional intelligence *'training'*, a term that applies to learning a skill rather than personal development, and which also implies a potential *'quick fix'* approach to becoming more emotionally intelligent. It's a bit like the motivational *'high'* that is often experienced after listening to an inspirational speaker, prompting a personal commitment (strong and genuine at the time!) to act on lessons learnt. Despite all those good intentions, what generally happens is that on return to the reality of dealing with the usual pressures in the work environment, commitments gradually fade away. So there's no *'quick fix'* to developing emotional intelligence – and it's about personal development and not *'training'*.

Emotional intelligence definitions

In simple terms, emotional intelligence is about acknowledging and understanding both our own and others' emotions, and dealing effectively with their impact by using appropriate approaches and behaviour. Before moving on to look at the benefits perceived by being more emotionally intelligent, its value in the working environment and most importantly its influence on both our psychological and physiological wellbeing, I will first offer an overview of the components and definitions put forward to describe the term.

The main components of emotional intelligence proposed by Daniel Goleman are: self-awareness, emotional management, self-motivation, empathy, managing relationships, communication skills and personal style. Goleman describes emotionally adept people as those who *'know and manage their own feelings well, and who deal effectively with other people's feelings'*.

Three key components of emotional intelligence proposed by Malcolm Higgs and Vic Dulewicz are:

- *Drivers* – the motivation and decisiveness that energise goal achievement

- *Constrainers* – the conscientiousness and integrity that facilitate the fit between principles, values and behaviour

- *Enablers* – the performance traits which contribute to success, such as sensitivity, influence and self-awareness.

And Malcolm Higgs suggests that emotional intelligence is: *'achieving one's goals through the ability to manage one's own feelings and emotions, be sensitive to and influence other key people, and balance one's own motives and drives with conscientious and ethical behaviour.'*

Emotional intelligence has also been described by Robert Cooper and Ayman Sawaf as *'the ability to sense, understand and effectively apply the power and acumen of emotions as a source of human energy, information, connection and influence'*; and by John Mayer and Peter

22

Salovey as *'the ability to perceive, to integrate, to understand and reflectively manage one's own and other people's feelings.'* The Mayer-Salovey model also defines emotional intelligence as *'the capacity to understand emotional information and to reason with emotions'*. More specifically, they divide emotional intelligence abilities into key areas in their *'four branch'* model as follows:

1. The capacity accurately to perceive emotions.
2. The capacity to use emotions to facilitate thinking.
3. The capacity to understand emotional meanings.
4. The capacity to manage emotions.

In a more recent paper, *'Emotional Intelligence Meets Traditional Standards for an Intelligence'*, John Mayer, David Caruso and Peter Salovey describe emotional intelligence as *'an ability to recognise the meanings of emotion and their relationships, and to reason and problem-solve on the basis of them.'* They continue: *'Emotional intelligence is involved in the capacity to perceive emotions, assimilate emotion-related feelings, understand the information of those emotions, and manage them.'* And according to Reuven Baron, emotional intelligence is defined as *'an array of non-cognitive capabilities, competencies, and skills that influence one's ability to succeed in coping with environmental demands and pressures.'* Dictionary definitions include: *'intelligence regarding the emotions, especially in the ability to monitor one's own or others' emotions.'*

So while there are lots of definitions and components varying in emphasis and expression, the core elements of emotional intelligence suggest an ability to:

- acknowledge and understand own body language and emotions.

- listen to and reflect on intuitive feelings (gut reactions).

- be aware of others' body language and behaviours, and interpret and anticipate their emotions.

- respond with appropriate behaviour to own and others' emotions within an ethical framework of principles and values.

It has however been argued by some, and particularly by critics of Daniel Goleman, that the meaning of the term has been embellished to include elements that were not part of the original Mayer and Salovey scientific construct (noting that the elements in their 4-branch model headings make no reference to ethics or integrity.) Should integrity (described as *'having the quality of strong moral principles'*) and morality (described as *'being concerned with the principles of right and wrong behaviour and the goodness or badness of human behaviour*) be omitted, you could argue that dictators such as Mussolini, Adolf Hitler and Saddam Hussein had *'emotional intelligence'*, in that they acknowledged and understood both their own and others' emotions. Whether they had *'strong moral principles'* is of course another question. But while integrity may not be explicit in a number of suggested definitions, emotional intelligence is however now generally understood to include a character based on an ethical framework of moral principles and values.

Following study of the emotional intelligence concept over the last 10 years, and the development of my resulting passion for its value, the definition I constructed in 1988 summarises elements as follows:

Emotional intelligence is:

'Acknowledging and understanding the influence of emotions on ourselves and others, and responding using integrity and intuition to guide behaviour'

And in the work that I do in developing emotionally intelligent leadership and teamwork, integrity is incorporated and emphasised as an intrinsic element of being emotionally intelligent. In defining a term that includes reference to a moral / ethical / integrity foundation, it could however be more accurately described as either *'moral based'* or *'integrity based'* emotional intelligence. My suggested term is *'ethical emotional intelligence'*, but for the purpose of using what has become a common expression, *'emotional intelligence'* (or EQ) is used throughout this book. Its intended meaning and its application however, incorporate both intuition and integrity.

To put the record straight about the terms *'emotional intelligence'* and *'emotional quotient'* and their abbreviations to either *'EI'* or *'EQ'*, the latter often tends to be used as preferred short term because it trips off the tongue more easily. (EI pronounced in a certain way can tend to sound a bit like a donkey noise imitation – which is a bit offputting!). EQ can also be understood to mean *'emotional competence'*, since the word *'quotient'*, more accurately relates to a level or measure. The more familiar term *'intellectual quotient'* (generally referred to as *'IQ'*) is the ratio of tested mental age to chronological age, usually expressed as a quotient multiplied by 100. The terms *'emotional intelligence'* or its abbreviation to *'EI'* and *'emotional quotient'* and its abbreviation to *'EQ'*, tend however to be used interchangeably.

Emotions versus feelings

A question that's sometimes asked in discussions about emotions, concerns the difference between emotions and feelings. One way to consider the distinction is the progression from thought to feeling, and then to emotion – while also recognising that only a limited number of thoughts that go through our minds then become a feeling, and then only a limited number of feelings progress to become an emotion. The difference could perhaps be described as progressive stages on a continuum according to degree of intensity; emotions not only being more intense but also longer lasting than thoughts or feelings.

It has even been estimated (although I'm not sure how the statistics were arrived at) that even when we're listening, as many as 7,200 thoughts per minute go through our minds! Emotions could therefore be described as being like *'stuck feelings'*, hence the tendency (as with 'EI' and 'EQ') for the terms *'feelings'* and *'emotions'* to be used interchangeably. What is also suggested is that the moment we try to *control* a feeling, we turn the feeling into an emotion.

Measuring EQ

Attempting to define someone's EQ level is another issue which opens a whole new debate that I don't intend to explore in depth in this book. Unlike an intelligence test that measures intellectual capability in (say) problem-solving or making mathematical calculations, it seems to me that while a judgement may be made according to the extent of a person's match with qualities, traits or behaviours perceived as *being* emotionally intelligent, actually defining a specific *level* of emotional intelligence has limited validity.

The various personality questionnaire type tests and others that have been devised can however be useful as guidelines in identifying typical situational responses and perceived personal effectiveness, including relative strengths, or areas where development may be needed to become more emotionally intelligent. And tests completed by those who know you well and are able to assess your typical situational responses are likely to have more credibility than those that are self-administered. The most convincing judgements are made when relevant behaviour traits are first self-assessed and then compared to others' views against the same criteria. Regardless of the method used, if people are consciously reflecting on their behaviour and aiming to develop their emotional intelligence as a result, then it's definitely a step in the right direction!

So, depending on your viewpoint, the meaning of emotional intelligence may seem either straightforward or complex, and you may or may not believe that a measure or quotient can be attributed. In any case, before the term emotional intelligence was defined the behaviours associated with its practice could be described as being mature, wise or having common sense – because, undoubtedly, being mature *(having reached a stage of mental or emotional development character of an adult)*, being wise *(having or showing experience, knowledge and good judgement)* and having common sense *(good sense and sound judgement in practical matters)* all relate to what is now generally recognised as being emotionally intelligent.

3

The Power of Emotions

'It is hard to overestimate the importance of
emotions in our lives – we organise our lives to
maximise the experience of positive emotions and
minimise the experience of negative emotions.'

Paul Ekman
(Author of *Emotions Revealed*)

Introducing emotional impact

The *Concise Oxford Dictionary* describes emotion as *'a strong feeling
such as joy, anger or sadness; an instinctive or an intuitive feeling as
distinguished from reasoning or knowledge'*, and *Encyclopaedia
Britannia* describes emotions as *'the synthesis of subjective
experience, expressive behaviour and neuro-chemical activity'*.
Words to describe emotions associated with being happy include:
ecstasy, bliss, contentment, wellbeing and joy. Words to express being
miserable or unhappy include: wretched, sad, downcast, dejected,
gloomy and melancholy. Terms to impart emotions associated with
anger include: fury, resentment, annoyance and indignation. We are,
however, more likely to notice our experience of negative emotions
associated with anger or anxiety rather than happiness because of
their generally more obvious and often instantaneous impact on our
bodies. Emotions such as anger, fear and anxiety trigger physiological

responses such as muscle tension, sweaty palms or *'tummy butterflies'* that we are immediately aware of. (More about emotions and the nervous system in the later chapter, *'Mind-Body Connection'*.)

Emotions – positive or negative?

We all experience a range of emotions; and they cannot simply be categorised into *'positive'* and *'negative'*. In the right circumstances, they all play a part in helping us to make sense of our experiences and the world we live in. It may however be helpful to highlight broad distinctions between emotions generally recognised as being either *'positive'* or *'negative'*, (i.e. perceived to have either a positive or negative psychological and/or physiological effect). For while it seems obvious that happiness is a positive emotion – along with others such as joy, love, hope and optimism – compassion and empathy are noted in particular as having both psychological and physiological beneficial effects and in making a key contribution towards having a positive outlook on life.

Negative emotions include: jealousy rage, guilt, depression and sadness. And while anger and fear are generally perceived as being 'negative' emotions with associated physiological consequences, nevertheless, depending on the circumstances, they could also be described as *'positive'* if, as a result of experiencing them, they are converted into commitment to take positive action. (The classic example is developing the attributes of an Olympic runner if you're being chased by a lion!). For instance, if our anger at injustice prompts action to deal with the perpetrators in a constructive way, then we can use what may be seen as a negative emotion to positive effect.

What is important in our day to day interactions with others, is being able to recognise any negative feelings that we or others are experiencing at an early stage. Developing an early stage awareness means we are better able to both manage our emotional responses to negative feelings and to deal more effectively with others. So becoming more attentive to both our own and others' emotions means we can learn to deal with them in more constructive ways. And consciously recognising what emotion a person may be feeling is a big step forward in improving our communication with them.

For a comprehensive list of emotions, the online encyclopedia, Wikipedia: http://en.wikipedia.org/wiki/List_of_emotions, currently lists 75 emotions, of which 58 are described in detail.

Positive and negative – situational examples

Emotions can be described as states of mind that result spontaneously from how we react to external or internal stimuli in the world around us. They also shape our subsequent responses to events and people, including the way we perceive ourselves. In *'Emotions Revealed'*, the world-renowned expert on body language, Paul Ekman, goes further in proposing that emotions actually determine the quality of our lives.

History gives us numerous and far reaching examples of the universal power of emotions associated with hate and anger that spill out in a dramatic way, resulting in death and destruction through war and conflict. And examples of positive emotions and their impact recognised at an international level include the love and compassion shown by Mother Teresa in the care and comfort of the poor in Calcutta, and the protracted struggle against apartheid in South Africa driven forward by the powerful influence of Nelson Mandela's resilience, tolerance, forgiveness and reconciliation.

Former British Prime Minister Margaret Thatcher once famously declared: *'There's no such thing as society'* (published in *Woman's Own*, October 1987). While her comment may have subsequently been taken out of context within the message of the reported interview, it ended up inadvertently being seen as encapsulating the political climate of the Eighties. I've referred to this well-known quotation because on a wider level in the society we live in (and there *is* such a thing as society!) we are also affected by the emotions and the resulting behaviour of those who have an impact on social order and the community at large.

Negative examples include the increasing problem of *'yob culture'*, generally attributed to a way of life that lacks respect for both people and property, where the behaviour of the young people involved results in distress and damage to communities and property – frequently blamed on circumstances such as lack of parental guidance, family breakdown, poverty, drug abuse, peer pressure or unemployment.

Positive examples include the contribution made by charities, community support groups and individuals, whose practical and emotional help makes such a beneficial difference to so many disadvantaged people in society. And not forgetting the countless numbers of family carers whose devotion to their loved ones encompasses emotional as well as practical support.

Emotional impact – summing up

So it's disrespect, indifference and cruelty, versus respect, kindness and compassion. Political, educational, economic and social investment in promoting and developing the latter and reducing or eliminating the former, would make a critical and far-reaching contribution towards the development of more caring communities and the wellbeing of wider society. At a political and practical level however, the focus of attention often seems to be on addressing the symptoms, rather than dealing with the causes of the underpinning negative emotions that influence the behaviour in the first place.

On a personal level, we don't need to be reminded how intense emotions such as love, sadness and anger impact on our lives. The joy and happiness of the birth of a much loved child, the sorrow and anguish of losing someone we love, or the anger and resentment felt when we are treated cruelly or contemptuously. The impact of the heartache of a broken relationship is even recognised in Germany as a quasi-medical condition (*'liebeskummer'*), with recognisable symptoms such as palpitations, nausea and irrational behaviour. Whether we acknowledge their impact or not, emotions are fundamental to every level of our lives – and their consequences affect us all. What is also of note, is that while others may be able to justify disagreement with facts we put forward, our feelings and emotions (should we choose to share these) cannot be refuted.

Self-esteem

> *'No one can make you feel inferior without your consent'*
>
> Eleanor Roosevelt
> (Wife of US President Franklin Roosevelt and
> outspoken advocate of human rights)

The power of emotions has a significant impact on our level of self-esteem – a term used to describe how a person feels about themselves in terms of their dignity, self-respect or self-worth. The two criteria generally used to assess self-esteem are:

1) self-recognition in terms of *characteristics* (e.g. attributes such as honesty, sense of fairness or sense of humour), and *capabilities* (such as professional ability or sporting talent); and

2) self-perception of *'loveworthiness'* – i.e. the value placed on self of being worthy of respect, being liked, loved and cared for by others.

Intrinsic belief in self-worth or value is, however, a subjective judgement. If this is easily affected by emotions associated with a belief in how others perceive you, then your self-esteem can be left in an unstable and vulnerable state. If conversely, self-esteem is maintained *despite* the way you are treated by others, you are more likely to retain emotional and therefore psychological stability.

The opposite of self-esteem is self-deprecation, where sense of self is perceived inferiority, and where for example, one's rights, beliefs, wants and needs are seen as less important than those of others. It is, however, important to distinguish between self-deprecation and being self-effacing. The former relates to belittling, whereas the latter is about modesty rather than denigration. The difference between self-deprecation and self-effacement is like making the distinction between the words *'arrogance'* and *'confidence'*. In terms of self-esteem, both self-deprecation and arrogance are seen as negative traits, whilst self-effacement and confidence are viewed as positive.

If we want to maximise our positive emotions as well as become more emotionally intelligent, an intrinsic sense of self-worth and an awareness and understanding of emotions and their impact on self and others are fundamental to the way we live. Being emotionally intelligent also requires a heightened sensitivity to others' emotions and a recognition that they too are striving to maximise the positive and minimise the negative according to the world that they experience.

The story of Viktor Frankl and the way he dealt with his incarceration as a Nazi prisoner of war is a supreme example of self-esteem and effective emotional management (as described in his book, *Man's Search for Meaning*). Despite being subjected to extremes of physical and psychological abuse and indignity, he focused on maintaining a high level of self-esteem and a meaning and purpose for his life. While physical mistreatment brings bodily pain, the most painful part of beatings he described as being *'the mental agony caused by the insults implied'*. In the face of mistreatment that most of us would only have in our worst nightmares, he maintained an emotional approach and an inner strength that he described as *'being able to retreat from terrible surroundings to a life of inner riches and spiritual freedom'*.

Emotions, intuition and decision-making

> *'We decide emotionally, then justify intellectually.'*
>
> Daniel Kahneman
> (Israeli born American and Professor of
> Psychology at Princeton University)

Emotions relate not only to our physiological and psychological wellbeing, but also to our decision-making and performance. Research into decision-making and its effectiveness suggests that many of the most highly skilled cognitive performances are intuitive, and that many complex, instinctive and speedy judgments are as effective as those made following detailed analysis. Albert Einstein also emphasised the link between intuition and decision-making in his assertion: *'There will come a point in everyone's life where only intuition can make the leap ahead, without ever knowing precisely how. One can never know why, but one must accept intuition as a fact.'*

Intuitive decision-making involves the adaptive unconscious part of our brain with the rapid data processing involved in making very quick judgements on little information – categorised by Gerd Gigerenzer as *'fast and furious'*, like being on *'automatic pilot'*. A more recent term for intuitive decision-making devised by Malcolm Gladwell and described in his bestselling book, *Blink*, is *'thin-slicing'*, i.e., the ability of our unconscious to find patterns in situations and behaviour based on very narrow slices of experience. Our thought processes, and any subsequent feelings and emotions associated with these, reverse back and forth between conscious and unconscious modes of thinking depending on the situation.

An ability to read people's body language, and the subtle (or sometimes more obvious!) messages we give out through our facial expressions, posture and general demeanour is intrinsic to intuitive thinking. This ability, allied with a pool of relevant knowledge and experience, plus the indefinable process of unconscious thought, is how effective intuitive thinkers make the right decisions.

Intuitive thinking is essential in conditions where rapid decision-making is vital for success, such as dealing with an immediately life-threatening situation. In the right circumstances, using our instinct also plays a significant part in achieving successful outcomes in both our professional and personal lives. For instance, an ability to rapidly recognise and understand our own and others' emotions and then deal with these effectively, can make the difference between building productive relationships, or dismantling them. So while successful decision-making most often relies on the appropriate balance between deliberate and instinctive thought processes, fine tuning and using intuitive thinking at a more conscious level can help you to make more effective decisions. And while I'm not proposing that you trust your instincts implicitly in every circumstance, I am suggesting that developing intuitive judgement not only contributes to decision-making in a range of situations, but also adds value to the practice of being more emotionally intelligent.

Integrity and emotional intelligence

The word integrity stems from the Latin *integritas*, and can be described as *'steadfast adherence to a strict moral or ethical code'* or *'the fit between principles, values and behaviour'*. In other words *'doing the right thing'* and holding yourself accountable for your actions.

So, you may ask, what's the difference between a principle and a value? As with 'EI' versus 'EQ', and *'emotions'* versus *'feelings'*, while there are subtle differences in interpretation, the terms tend to be used interchangeably because of overlaps in the substance of their meanings. To clarify the distinction between them, principles can be seen as fundamental general truths, basic tenets or moral codes – such as a rule of law concerning natural phenomena, a system or a guiding theory – whereas values represent discrete personal differences between people in the views they hold as unique and distinctive individuals.

By examining, clarifying and articulating the values we believe in, we give voice to our conscience – the sense of right or wrong that influences our thoughts and behaviour. If we are committed to and governed by our values, then they act as the fundamental premise to what we think, say and do, and are the restrainers or drivers that influence our behaviour. Amongst others, values that support emotionally intelligent behaviour include: self-respect, respect for others, openness, honesty, self-awareness, an openness to learning and a willingness to change. The principles and values that influence our thoughts and behaviour – and our reference to them as guidelines in the way that we manage our emotions (as well as recognise and deal with others' emotions and behaviour) – are therefore fundamental to EQ, or what could more accurately be described as *'ethical emotional intelligence'*.

4

Why EQ is Important

'Reaching a state of freedom as regards emotions does
not mean being apathetic or insensitive – it simply
means that, instead of always being the plaything of our
negative thoughts, moods and temperaments, we
become their masters.'

Matthieu Ricard
(French born Buddhist and author, noted for
connecting western science with Buddhist philosophy)

Introduction

Our emotions and the emotions of others impact on every aspect of
our lives. Our own emotions direct our moods, impact on our self-
esteem and influence our interactions with others at work, at home
and in society. They also have a major affect on our level of
motivation – i.e. whether or not we *want* to do things or not. (At
home: Am I in the mood to wash the car / mop the floor / walk the
dog? At work: Am I inspired to write this report / deal with this
customer / work with this team?) But it's not just our own emotions
we need to understand and deal with. It's also about relating to others
by understanding them and by recognising how they might be feeling
– and then engaging with them in an appropriate way. So, whether we
consciously recognise it or not, how we manage our own emotions
and whether we relate to others in an emotionally intelligent way has
a major influence on our lives.

While it may be obvious that having loving and rewarding

relationships play a key part in whether or not we have a fulfilling personal life, our success in the workplace is also significantly dependent on whether or not we have productive working relationships with our colleagues, our boss and others we connect with. So our level of emotional competence makes a key contribution to whether we build or dismantle both business and social relationships, and as such has important consequences to both our work and personal lives.

The first and most important relationship, fundamental to being emotionally intelligent, is the one with self. Like the proverbial iceberg, there's far more beneath the surface than above it, and we need to relate to this – the unseen thoughts we have in our minds that govern our self-perception, our observation of others and the way we behave as a result. Perception of self-worth, i.e. level of self-esteem, and being self-assured and confident (*'comfortable in our own skin'*) is the foundation on which we can then go on to build effective relationships with others. If on the other hand, our self-perception is one of inferiority and insecurity, or conversely of superiority over others, in either case we're unlikely to effectively engage with people and go on to build successful relationships.

A high level of emotional intelligence also contributes to effective management of stress, whether at work or at home. Successful stress management relates particularly to positive emotions, (such as self-confidence, hope and trust), attributes (such as tolerance, an optimistic outlook and a calm disposition) and abilities (such as self-awareness, self-acceptance and an openness to learn) – along with making perceptive and balanced judgements on what *can* and *can't* be changed.

A further reason why EQ is important is the connection between mind, body and emotions and the links between our psychological and physiological wellbeing. Increasing recognition of the relationship between positive thoughts and emotions and the resulting beneficial effect on the immune system and general wellbeing, is now a rapidly emerging field of study, referred to as psychoneuro-immunology   (More about this in the chapter on *'Emotions and Mind-Body Connection'*.)

Achieving an effective work/life balance is also often quoted as an ideal we should strive for. Since the majority of us spend a significant proportion of our lives at work in any case, I have, however, never understood the distinction implied between *'work'* and *'life'*. The following two sections highlight the importance of emotional intelligence to both our work and personal lives, with broad distinctions made between *'work life'* – meaning the time we actually spend in the workplace or involved in activities related to work – and *'personal life'* – the time we spend outside the work environment. Since the principles and practice of emotional intelligence remain the same whether we are at work or away from the workplace, the distinction is made only for purposes of emphasis in the key messages involved.

A final note on the introduction to why EQ is important – when we truly and deeply reflect on aspects of our lives that are important, it's generally the investment in relationships and the lack of time and effort we have made in these that are cause for regret, rather than achievements that relate to material outcomes.

Work life impact

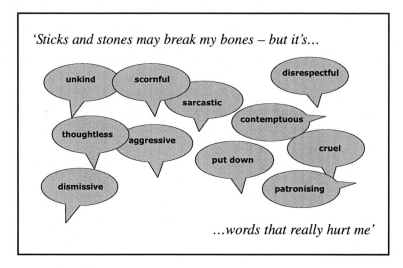

'Sticks and stones may break my bones – but it's...

unkind   scornful

disrespectful

sarcastic

contemptuous

thoughtless   aggressive

cruel

put down

dismissive   patronising

...words that really hurt me'

The above adaptation from the well-known children's rhyme, replacing the original *'words will never hurt me'*, will be well recognised by those who have received a tongue lashing, sarcastic comments or destructive (rather than constructive) criticism. An example of the power of words to have a profoundly damaging psychological impact, was tellingly reported by Stephen Fry, the actor and TV personality, when he attributed a key factor influencing his depression and suicide attempts, to being tormented by poor reviews of the West End play *'Cell Mates'* that he starred in. So whether words are written or spoken, if they are unkind, scornful, sarcastic or contemptuous, they can have harmful and intense consequences to the recipient's wellbeing as well as to human relationships whether at work or at home.

Non-communication can be equally destructive. Being deliberately ignored when you say something, being intentionally shut out of a conversation, or someone purposefully avoiding eye contact in order to demonstrate a lack of recognition or respect, are just three examples. And bullying behaviour involving subtle, insidious and sarcastic words is just as damaging as physically aggressive bullying. So bullying is clearly as much about psychological harm as it is about as physical violence.

Communicating effectively within the workplace is undoubtedly emotionally intelligent. What may not always be recognised, however, is the impact that effective communication of all types has on productivity and on profits as well as people's wellbeing. Research findings show that that effective communication is a leading indicator of an organisation's financial performance and profits. Research also indicates that on average, firms within the financial and retail trade sectors are ranked among the most effective communicators; whilst healthcare, telecommunications and other service companies rank among the least effective.

A study carried out by Surcon International in 2004 suggested that up to 50% of an organisation's productivity is predictable based on employees' feelings and opinions. According to surveys, up to 85% of people believe they could double their productivity ... *'if they wanted to'.*...and they don't want to, with survey results citing lack of effective leadership as the key reason for lack of motivation and its negative impact on productivity. And a more recent survey of 2,000 employees, sponsored by the Chartered Institute of Personnel and Development (CIPD) and carried out by Kingston Business School (reported in *People Management,* December 2006) suggested that the relationships between employers and employees in many British workplaces are like *'marriages under stress'.* Dissatisfaction with their relationships with their managers was highlighted by 43% of employees, with 30% of respondents noting that they rarely or never received feedback on their performance (either constructive or otherwise). The overall conclusion was that lack of effective communication and low levels of trust between bosses and staff was leading to underperformance and low productivity.

So the way people are treated in the workplace by their leaders and managers can have a significant impact on their motivation, and subsequently on their contribution to organisational performance. On this basis, if high level EQ were to become the general behaviour pattern between people in the workplace (with an emphasis on underpinning integrity), then it seems obvious that the work

45

environment would not only be more understanding and caring but also more productive. And since being emotionally intelligent means having the ability to manage one's own emotions and deal with others more effectively, handling potentially stressful situations will also be less problematic. The ability to manage feelings and handle stress is therefore a key aspect of emotional intelligence, fundamental to success in the workplace.

'If you want to do a job without stress – become a dinner lady or accountant,' was a news headline in The Times on January 15th 2005. Whether the majority of dinner ladies (and shouldn't it be dinner men or ladies, in any case?) and accountants would agree is likely to be another matter. Interestingly, *'emotional labour'* was noted as an important facet of the experience of occupational stress, with jobs that require a need to hide true feelings and emotions highlighted as being the most stressful. These included occupations such as ambulance crew, teachers, social workers, call centre employees, prison officers, police and clerical/administrative staff. What is also interesting was the emphasis by the researchers that nursing, a job with high emotional content, was not included in the top seven stressful occupations.

While lots of research still needs to be done into EQ in the workplace, evidence to date indicates that the work life impact of emotional intelligence, or its absence, is significant. In parallel with their personal lives, people want to be respected, valued, and communicated with effectively at work, and the relationships they have with others in their working environment are important to them. Leaders and managers evidently play a key role in whether or not emotionally intelligent behaviour is part of the culture of an organisation. Listening to and valuing people, keeping them informed and giving constructive feedback, are just a few examples of how leaders can be emotionally intelligent.

But it's not just managers who have an influence; it's also about the people who work together in groups or teams. If productive relationships and valued and trusted teamwork are dominant at work, and the focus is on a shared commitment to achieve, then open and honest dialogue is encouraged and time-wasting through political manoeuvring can be significantly reduced and even eliminated. If the opposite is true, and building productive relationships and working interdependently across the organisation is not seen as important, the climate is likely to be one of competition rather than collaboration between functions and roles.

Most organisations fall somewhere between the two, and are in any case involved in a continuing process of changing organisational dynamics and cultural shifting. A recognition that happier employees equals higher productivity means, however, that commercial considerations, not just employers' altruism, will drive the workplace wellbeing agenda. Should the executive leadership of *'UK plc'* openly recognise, value and invest in the development of emotionally intelligent behaviour (including their own!), as well as deal effectively with the damaging impact of its absence, then this would make a major contribution to workplace wellbeing and thus to productivity. And since most of us spend a significant proportion of our lives at work (and even if not working we are in any case are in frequent contact with those who are), then we would all reap the benefit.

Personal life impact

> '*How different our lives are when we really know what is deeply important to us, and keeping that picture in mind, we manage ourselves each day to be and to do what really matters most.*'
>
> Stephen Covey
> (Author of *The Seven Habits of Highly Effective People*)

Building and maintaining meaningful and rewarding personal relationships is the essence of being human. And while most of us spend a significant proportion of our waking life at work, the relationships we have with close family and friends are the ones that touch us most deeply on an emotional level. While work achievements or other interests we are passionate about may be significant to us, the chances are, when asked what is most important the majority of us will put other people first on the list, such as family and friends. And unless by some chance we are suffering from a severe psychotic disorder that reduces or eliminates emotional feelings, emotions will be involved.

The perception of immortality we have when we are young – and the far distant horizon of middle age (old age at the time, is of course an unthinkable impossibility!) – mutates as we grow older, into a developing and heightened conscious recognition that one day we will no longer exist as living, breathing human beings. And as we grow older, we also come to value our relationships more. In my own case, with mortality awareness now firmly established, although relationships have been important to me for as long as I can remember, their relative significance and the value I attach to them have grown along with advancing years.

The most moving and inspiring book I read in 2006, was *Chasing Daylight: How My Forthcoming Death Transformed my Life*, written by Eugene O'Kelly, the late chairman and chief executive of KPMG (USA). When diagnosed with brain cancer in May 2005 and given only three months to live, Eugene O'Kelly made a momentous psychological shift in focus, and turned from dealing with the challenges of business, to prioritising the time investment he had left according to the importance of his relationships with others.

Despite its message, he described the verdict of his terminal condition as *'turning out to be a gift'* because it inspired a new level of awareness of what was important in his life. Along with his heightened awareness, he instigated a plan to invest the time he had left in doing what he described as *'Closing the circle'* with the people who had been part of his life. To *'close the circle'*, he strived to connect with as many people as possible, to share his thoughts, memories and gratitude for the times they had shared. Although working relationships were important, and many working relationships had also become significant personal relationships, those that were first and foremost on the priority list were naturally his family and closest friends.

> *'I was blessed. I was told I had three months to live.'*
>
> Eugene O'Kelly
> (Author of *Chasing Daylight*)

Eugene O'Kelly's story is inspiring not only because of his emphasis on the importance of relationships and the value of investing time and effort in them, but also because its message reinforces the importance of focusing on and enjoying living in the moment. I find it particularly moving that not only did he work towards effectively *'closing the circle'* of his relationships – he also made the momentous effort to write the book. His hope was that by sharing his experience he would inspire others not only to make the most of life, but also to reduce the fear of facing its end.

The important personal questions

So the first question to ask in considering the impact of emotional intelligence on your personal life is:

- Who are the people most important to you?

And the second question is:

- How often do you reflect on this and invest time and effort accordingly in building and maintaining effective relationships with them?

There are of course lots of additional questions relating to awareness and understanding of one's own and others' emotions and the principles and values that guide behaviour, but these are the two key questions to keep in mind in reflecting on the personal life impact of emotional intelligence. And while any lack of emotional intelligence we experience in our working lives has repercussions, its impact is even more intense if things go wrong with our intimate personal relationships. The expression, *'It's words that really hurt me'*, obviously applies especially to these – to the people we are closest to and care most deeply about.

The significance of trust

> *'To be trusted is a greater compliment than being loved.'*
>
> George Macdonald
> (Scottish author, poet and Christian minister)

Trust is the intangible but critical constituent that binds effective relationships together, and it is fundamental to successful communications in both our personal and working lives. Having close, trusted and valued personal relationships is at the very essence of human wellbeing. And high-level trust in any teamwork situation enables the leader and his or her team to achieve maximum productivity by focusing on interdependent task achievement. Without trusted engagement, the danger is that in both our work and personal lives, we become sidetracked into potentially damaging relationship issues. So to develop and maintain meaningful personal relationships and to achieve leadership and team performance excellence, trust is essential.

Exceptional levels of trust, team excellence and ultimate interdependency are required for high-risk circumstances such as military combat, search-and-rescue and aerobatics (the RAF *'Red Arrows'* display team are a classic example), or in situations such as complex heart or brain surgery. But what does trust mean in the day-to-day work environment outside these extremes, and how does it affect leaders and teams?

Trust is having reliance on and confidence in the integrity of the people you work with. It means that the principles and values that they operate by and the behaviours associated with these are in line with yours. If there is a high level of trust between leaders and their teams, first and foremost there will be a belief in others' authenticity – a confidence that there is a genuine match between the integrity they espouse and what they actually do. Expected behaviours include being open and honest, respecting and valuing others and keeping confidences: *'Say what you mean, and mean what you say.'* High-level trust also means sharing opinions openly and honestly, giving and receiving constructive feedback and providing appropriate practical and emotional support.

The more we trust an individual or a group, the more we are likely to share with them the depth and scope of our feelings and any emotions associated with these. This means of course, there is a powerful connection between the degree of emotionally intelligent behaviour in place amongst the people concerned and the extent to which they trust each other.

5

Emotions and Mind-Body Connection

> 'The body expresses what the mind represses.'
>
> Dr Paddy Welles
> (American marriage and family therapist)

Introduction

Emotions are part of our survival mechanism as human beings, an intrinsic part of being human. Every emotion creates a reaction – the type and intensity dependent on a complex range of factors and their context. Feelings such as anger, sadness and fear produce a range of body reactions with varying degrees of potency depending on the situation we're in and the distinctive and intensely personal way we experience these. If you've just been subjected to what you consider an unjustified (and possibly aggressively delivered) dressing-down from your boss and you're feeling angry or upset as a result, you're more than likely to take it out on the next person you come across. Whereas if you've just received deserved praise for work well done, the odds are that the next person you communicate with will get the benefit of your positive state of mind and the warm glow you're likely to be feeling as a result. And the chances are that in either case, people will have an idea of your mood and what you may be thinking by your expression.

Body language indicators

Silvan Tomkins, the late American personality theorist, once began a lecture by bellowing, *'The face is like the penis!'* Not the lecture introduction the students expected, but it succeeded in getting their immediate attention! Their body language responses, including amusement, surprise (and probably some embarrassment), were indicated by the looks on their faces – which was of course the point Silvan Tomkins was making. What he meant by noting the similarity, was that our involuntary facial expressive system is the way we disclose our emotions, and that to a large extent, the face also has a mind of its own.

Paul Ekman, the psychologist and renowned world expert on body language says that basic emotions are hard to conceal because of what he described as *'micro-expressions'*, i.e. those lasting for less than a second that are under the control of the subconscious. For instance, in a demonstration delivered for the police and MI6, he showed that expert face-readers can pinpoint in seconds when someone is telling lies through being able to read facial expressions.

The eyes in particular, said to be the *'windows of the soul'*, play a key part in expressing emotion. In contrast to an insincere or polite smile, sometimes described as *'professional'* or *'Pan American'* (after the former airline of the same name), a genuine involuntary smile of real happiness or pleasure engages both mouth and eye muscles and is noticeable to an acute observer. But our spontaneous facial expressions and other body language indicators also provide important signals of our authentic feelings. They can help to inform our decisions in dealing with our emotional experiences, and also give indications about our feelings towards others.

Dealing with stress

Throughout our lives, we all have to deal with a range of stressors, yet as individuals we differ dramatically in our vulnerability to their impact because of the way that we deal with them. A significant change of thinking in the medical world about the importance of emotions has evolved over recent years as a result of increasing and compelling evidence of the relationship between emotional and physical health. Links between the mind (psychology), the brain (neurology) and the body's natural defence system (immunology) form a rapidly emerging field of study, referred to as psychoneuroimmunology, and research results indicate that the mind-body connection and its impact on our immune system as well as our energy levels can be profound.

The brain and the body interact to produce emotions and their expression, often seemingly totally outside our control or influence. For instance, when we're feeling anxious, a typical physiological response we experience is *'butterflies in the tummy'* – aptly expressed by Enoch Powell, the late politician, in his well-known quote: *'When I repress my emotion my stomach keeps score.'*

The onset of a stress response is associated with specific physiological actions in the sympathetic nervous system, which consists of cells, tissues, and organs that regulate the body's responses to internal and external stimuli. In vertebrates it consists of the brain, spinal cord, nerves, ganglia, and parts of the receptor and effector organs. And if a neuron has been sparked by particularly intense thought, the result is a pulse of electricity which then releases chemical messengers referred to as neurotransmitters. Stressful and intense emotions such as fear, anger or rage result in hyper-limbic system activity, in what the neurologist and physiologist Walter Cannon termed the *'fight or flight'* response, also referred to as the *'acute stress response'*. Increases in heart rate and breathing, perspiration and muscle tension are some of the more obvious changes that we can sense that occur directly as a result of emotional impact. And to deal with a stressful situation on a psychological level, we tend to narrow our focus to concentrate on the perceived danger and effect and shut out anything that distracts from this. Hence the way those who are unable to control their temper tend to lash out either physically or verbally, without thinking about the wider environment or the potential consequences of their behaviour.

A large percentage of stress related diseases are thought to be disorders of the autonomic nervous system caused by the impact of excessive and prolonged negative stress responses. If you therefore repeatedly turn on stress responses and cannot turn these off after the event, there can be longer-term health repercussions.

Positive psychological influences can, however, reduce the negative physiological impact when we are dealing with a stressful situation. What is important in effectively handling stressful situations is not just focusing on the external reality of the situation, but choosing the meaning we attach to it and the emotional response we formulate as a result. By developing a deeper understanding of our emotions and learning to deal with them in productive ways and positively influencing our thoughts, feelings, emotions and moods, we can optimise our coping strategies for handling stressful situations. So an ability to respond to challenging situations in a calm and rational way limits the potential for experiencing an intense and negative emotional response, and means that we're less likely to be vulnerable to potentially damaging physiological reactions.

The memory impact

But when we feel any emotion strongly enough, we tend to make decisions without processing information rationally, relying instead on learned experiences and stereotypes to make judgements in how we deal with them. What is significant is that intense thought and its physiological impact relate not only to the experience of the moment, but also to recollection of events from the past and the emotions associated with these. And the limbic system also influences the formation of memory by integrating emotional states with stored memories of physical sensations.

The memories we hold from past experiences that have touched us deeply in an emotional sense can be recalled to replicate the same emotions and physical reactions in new but similar scenarios. It's like holding your new grandchild and going back emotionally to the same situation with your own child and experiencing the same warm and loving physical sensations. Or it may be remembering the rage you felt (but may not have expressed) when you were bullied years ago, and when you're in a new situation when you think this could be happening again, feeling the same emotions welling up inside you along with the same internal muscle tension.

Despite the belief which many people seem to have that they are unable to change, neuroscientists confirm that the brain has inherent capacity to adapt (scientifically referred to as brain *'plasticity'*), through its ability to grow new neural connections. So retaining positive memories and the emotions associated with these, and choosing to adjust stored responses of negative experiences to more positive emotions, is within our capacity as human beings.

Compassion – and conclusions

Scientific evidence also recognises the physical and emotional benefits resulting from compassionate states of mind. Positive emotions such as joy, confidence and empathy have been found not only to contribute towards a state of personal happiness and wellbeing, but also to release hormones that have a beneficial effect on the immune system. So *'inner transformation'* can be achieved through cultivating thoughts towards more uplifting emotions. Even *'acting'* happy by consciously smiling has been shown to influence feelings of happiness – a worthwhile incentive to think positively both about past experiences as well as the moment we're living in.

The good news, therefore, is that influencing our thoughts towards the development of more positive and inspiring emotions has a beneficial effect on our physical condition. Emotions consequently don't just shape our ability to understand ourselves and relate to other people; they also affect our health. And future research concerning neurological cognitive processes – how the brain actually works and how these processes relate to emotional impact – will undoubtedly make a further contributions towards our understanding of emotional intelligence.

> *'The human mind is 90 per cent of the game of life. By achieving mastery over your thoughts, emotional and physical states can be influenced and performance can be maximised.'*
>
> Nick Bollettieri
> (Renowned tennis coach, credited with developing many world class champions)

6

Negative and Positive EQ Practice

Introduction

Every day, news items include reports and articles that arouse a range of emotions. The anger felt by fox hunting supporters on the introduction of a law banning its practice (contrasting with the pleasure of anti-hunting lobbyists), the distress of NHS patients having to wait for operations or unable to get the drugs they need, and the despair and anger of people subjected to continuing anti-social behaviour, are just a few examples. Emotions likely to be more widely felt include compassion for people suffering from starvation or disease (along with anger and frustration that this is still happening in the 21st century), or concern at the issues arising from global warming.

The following reported news items are likely to have resulted in a range of negative emotions in people who have strong views about the issues raised, as well as the people directly affected:

- published reports of corporate financial misconduct in major corporations such as Enron, Andersen, Parmalat and Boeing.

- the naming of high-street chains Dixons, Currys, Comet, Sony, Halifax, Ikea and others as culprits of misleading practices of by the National Consumer Council (NCC).

- recent reports on internal memos at British American Tobacco (BAT) stating that their real aim was to promote smoking to young people, contrary to their published policy of pushing for a minimum age for tobacco sales.

- the story of the Merrill Lynch lawyer *'hounded out'* of his job after blowing the whistle on the investment bank's alleged mismanagement of some of Britain's biggest pension funds.

- the paying of an additional £4M towards a directors' retirement benefits trust fund by loss making company MG Rover.

So what's this got to do with emotional intelligence you may ask? While these are evidently stories about questionable judgement or integrity, the executives involved also displayed a lack of emotional intelligence in the decisions they made and in the actions they carried out, sanctioned or condoned. For while emotional intelligence is clearly involved in direct communication with people, its practice relates not only to engagement with individuals or groups, but also to executive decisions about policy and strategy and how the results of their implementation impact on people. In the examples highlighted, job losses, overpriced goods, plummeting share prices and ill health were some of the direct results. There were a number of groups of people likely to feel extreme negative emotions as a result of the announcements: clients, shareholders, employees and parents (in the case of BAT), as well as interested members of the general public. The chairman of MG Rover, John Towers, at the time of the above news item in October 2004, was even reported as *'driving his employees to emotional extremes'*.

The classic and often quoted business example that effectively demonstrates a singular lack of emotional intelligence is, however, Gerald Ratner's comment made in his speech at the Institute of Directors' dinner in 2001, when he described his company's sherry decanters as *'total crap'*. An ill-judged comment that he's never been allowed to forget! Denigrating the company's goods not only offended shareholders and staff, but was also an insult to the customers putting money in the tills. The result was the loss of an estimated £500 million off the company's stockmarket valuation, and the loss of his own job and his personal fortune.

Another telling, although not so dramatic, example of the absence of emotional intelligence is the study into the identification of doctors most likely to be sued by their patients for medical malpractice (referred to in Malcolm Gladwell's book, *Blink*). In telling the story, it was emphasised that the issues taken up by patients did not relate directly to how they were operated on and the success or otherwise of their operations, but on the *relationships* patients had with their doctors. The study found that doctors least likely to be sued were those who treated their patients effectively on a personal level – in other words, treated them with respect, and made the effort to listen to, understand them and recognise how they might be feeling.

On the other hand, patients who reported malpractice said that they were rushed, ignored or treated poorly in some way, and felt they did not have a good relationship with their doctor. These patients said that they were not looked at as a whole person, not listened to and their questions were not answered. Generally, not enough time was spent communicating with them. What was reported to be most offensive, was being talked down to and not treated with respect, with the doctor's tone of voice referred to as a key indicator.

More illustrations follow of either emotional intelligence or its absence, in a range of contexts varying from a public library (positive example) to a high street bank and a nursing home (negative examples). We start with examples of the *absence* of emotional intelligence, and in all these cases it is evident that if emotionally intelligent practice *had* been in place, not only would this have benefited relationships between the people concerned and their wellbeing, but in many cases it would also have had more positive outcomes in terms of productivity and profitability. Each of the following case studies concludes with the key EQ message that comes out of the story.

61

Non EQ Examples

The bungling bank

'Abuse of power – bank fails a caring daughter' was the newspaper headline reporting on Barclays Bank employees' bungling in dealing with a simple case of identity (The Times – 10.1.04).

When Ada Evans, formerly a fiercely independent 87-year-old had a fall resulting in a diminished mental state, her daughter Linda reluctantly had her admitted to a residential home. Prior to her fall, Ada had taken a particular pride in retaining control over her investments, but as a result of her new situation, chose to sign over control of her finances to her daughter. Power of attorney was subsequently signed over to Linda in a straightforward process duly dealt with by their solicitor. However, the process of becoming a signatory to her mother's Barclays Bank account, which should therefore have been simple to arrange, ended up being a costly, upsetting and time wasting process because of bank staff's ineptitude.

In common with many professional women, Linda Evans retained her maiden name for work purposes, but used her married name for her driving licence and bank accounts. In an attempt to make it easier for the bank, Linda signed the required bank form in both names, taking with her as identity evidence, her marriage and birth certificates and her driving licence. However, because the address on the power of attorney document was not identical to that on her bank statement, bank staff refused the application.

The next day, Linda's husband then dutifully brought in a utility bill showing a matching address, but he was turned away because his wife had not signed with her middle initial. So the following day, Linda then returned to the bank and duly signed the form again using her middle initial as required. Enough evidence now for Linda to prove she was who she said she was? No; because a week later, Barclays contacted Linda again, to ask why she had not used her married name in her passport.

By now, Linda was becoming increasingly exasperated at what was a distressing time both for her and the family. But when Linda tried to contact the bank's customer services and public relations departments to find out why there was a delay, no response was forthcoming. The bank eventually responded, however, to advise that her mother's signature had now been lost, and would her mother mind *'popping into the branch'* to provide another one? Should her mother have been able to do this, she would of course not have needed her daughter to be a signatory. All very obvious really! – And a request clearly not in the best interests of good public relations. It subsequently took the bank over eight weeks to deal properly with Linda, albeit with an apology for their poor service and £50 to make up for the interest she had lost because of having to fund her mother's residential home fees in the interim.

The story of Linda Evans and the way she was treated shows a demonstrable lack of basic common sense by the bank staff in recognising and understanding what emotions may be involved. What is also surprising is that amongst the staff involved in dealing with her, no one seemed to question the impact on their customer service reputation and how this might affect business.

EQ message: Engage with the customer

When Linda Evans first went to the bank after obtaining power of attorney, a lack of emotional intelligence from bank staff was evident from the word go. While money-laundering checks are recognised as being standard banking procedure, the seemingly zealous way in which this was carried out resulted in making a stressful situation for the customer worse rather than better.

Dealing with Linda in a more considerate way by being mindful of her likely emotional state while still carrying out necessary checks, would have made so much difference both to customer wellbeing and to the bank's reputation, not forgetting the time and other resources that were also wasted all round.

The 'Care Plan Funeral' or 'Not Dead Yet!'

The word *'care'* in the Collins English Dictionary, is described as: *'to be troubled or concerned; be affected emotionally; to have regard or consideration'*. These were certainly not the principles applied in the following communication approach used by a Midlands nursing home, when supposedly adhering to the Commission for Social Care requirements:

DEAR...........

AS INSTRUCTED BY THE COMMISSION FOR SOCIAL CARE INSPECTION, IT IS A REQUIREMENT OF THE HOME TO HAVE PERSONAL DETAILS REGARDING FUNERAL ARRANGEMENTS INCLUDED IN THE RESIDENT'S CARE PLAN. THEREFORE, I WOULD BE VERY GRATEFUL IF YOU WOULD COMPLETE AND RETURN THE ATTACHED FORM. IF YOU HAVE ANY QUERIES, PLEASE DO NOT HESITATE TO CONTACT ME.

YOURS SINCERELY

What's so unreasonable about a letter like that that, you may ask. The above is reproduced verbatim and in its entirety from the nursing home concerned. (And yes, it was also all written in upper case!) So why shouldn't nursing home management with residents who may be seriously ill and could die whilst in their care have information about funeral arrangements?

But how are you likely to feel if you're an elderly lady with your husband in a nursing home, and you get this letter? After all, he'd been in the nursing home for several months, and when you visited him the day before you received the letter he seemed fine – and none of the staff had said anything to you. The first thought when this happened to the lady concerned, was that he must have died. Not difficult to imagine the emotions involved and their impact on an elderly person. As it turned out, her husband hadn't died. In fact despite his illness, he was keeping reasonably well.

EQ message: Consider emotional impact – and show empathy

While it may be helpful and even necessary for nursing home management to have knowledge of any proposed funeral arrangements for residents who may die whilst in their care, there are clearly more sensitive, emotionally intelligent approaches that could have been taken to find this out.

Had the management and staff involved given any thought and concern as to what people's feelings might be on receiving such a letter, a totally different and much more caring approach would have been used. A standard letter, which this was, with the addressee's name handwritten and a *'per pro'* signature on behalf of the matron, is distinctly not the right method.

In this case, in a situation which is clearly likely to be very upsetting, a more appropriate way would have been to have a sensitive one-to-one discussion. What is also important is that the tone as well as the content of the discussion should show compassion and care. And should written communication be necessary regarding such a sensitive issue, at the very least it would appear more compassionate if this is actually signed by the sender.

So, the message here for management and staff seeking information from people about personal issues that are likely to be distressing, is to give conscious thought about potential emotional impact and only *after* this consideration, choose an appropriate way to communicate.

The line manager bully

> *'Most organisations have a serial bully. It never ceases to amaze me how one person's divisive, disordered, dysfunctional behaviour can permeate the entire organisation like a cancer.'*
>
> Tim Field
> (Author of *Bully in Sight* and founder of the UK National Bullying Advice Line)

An obvious example of non EQ behaviour is bullying, whether it takes the form of physical or psychological aggression. Research in 2003 by the Department for Education and Skills and the charity Childline found that 51% of primary and 54% of secondary pupils thought bullying was a problem in their school. And in the workplace, a survey undertaken the same year by IRS Employment found that bullying had ousted pay as the top complaint by all workers, with 45% of the total complaints made relating to harassment and bullying. Within the public sector in particular, evidence of bullying was noted as being on the increase throughout, and especially in the NHS where managers were under pressure to deliver government targets (as reported by Lyn Witheridge, chief executive of the Andrea Adams Trust, the anti-bullying organisation)

The late Dr Tim Field founded the UK National Bullying Advice Line following his own experience of workplace bullying and the damaging personal consequences he suffered as a result. From his research into bullying, he found there was a generic pattern in all bullying cases, along with typical characteristics of perpetrators and victims. He identified thirteen types of workplace bullying described variously as: pressure, organisational, corporate, institutional, client, serial, secondary, pair, gang, vicarious, regulation, residual, and cyber.

Bullying, whatever its type and whether physical or psychological, generally takes place where there is an imbalance of power (or perceived power) between the parties concerned. And while children's experience of bullying can frequently include both physical and verbal abuse, within the workplace bullying often takes the form of psychological abuse through the bully seeking to intimidate or humiliate others in subtle and underhand ways. Intimidation and control through scare tactics and oppression that may not include actual bodily assault by the perpetrator can also result in visible damage to the victim, such as physical exhaustion and illness, as well as the more obvious psychological stress.

But while psychological bullying may not always result in obvious physical and visible damage to the victims, it is nevertheless insidious in all its forms because of the covertly aggressive approach used by its perpetrators. Overt or covert sarcasm, indirect or more obvious put-downs and sexist or racially abusive comments are typical behaviours of the psychological bully.

The emotional damage of experiencing psychological bullying includes intense feelings of resentment, anger and hurt, very often allied with a lack of self-esteem which subsequently makes it more difficult to deal with its effects. People who are confident and assertive are generally more able to deal effectively with this form of bullying, and are often able to limit the likelihood of future attempts because of the way they handle it.

The abuse of workplace power superiority can, though, be challenging and stressful to deal with, however assertive you are in addressing it. And the damage caused by bullying goes much wider and deeper than just with the victims and their personal emotional experiences. Longer-term repercussions can not only affect victims' health and wellbeing, but also impact on family, colleagues and others who suffer the negative effects resulting from the sufferers' changed behaviour. But bullying can also result in significant hurt to the pocket of the perpetrators as well as damage to the victims.

Take the case of Hull City Council, who in 2004 were forced to pay out £10,000 for the stress, humiliation and *'psychiatric damage'* suffered by one of their employees, Christopher Dunnachie who was bullied by his line manager. In all, Dunnachie was awarded the maximum £51,700 payout for his economic loss as well as being bullied. The headline *'Bullying case could trigger a torrent of payout claims'* in the Sunday Times should have rung alarm bells not only throughout public sector management, but to everyone in a management role.

While the total monetary payout to Christopher Dunnachie may seem relatively insignificant in relation to the council's overall budget, staff time and the more difficult to measure lost productivity costs are the *'hidden expenses'* incurred, not to mention the legal costs involved. Overall legal costs included not just those associated with the initial court ruling, but a subsequent Court of Appeal ruling, followed by a further ruling in the House of Lords which overturned the previous Court of Appeal decision! So lots of money spent in going through the due legal process. And all because of inappropriate behaviour meted out by a manager towards a member of staff.

EQ message: Build and maintain productive working relationships based on mutual respect.

Hull City Council is clearly not the only employer to have problems with bullying; and bullying by managers towards their subordinates is not the only problem – it's also a dilemma when it occurs between colleagues. Workplace bullying is a growing issue that is currently estimated to cost the UK economy £4 billion in sick leave, law suits, lost productivity and staff replacement costs. So investing time and effort in bullying prevention contributes not only to people's wellbeing but pays off in increased productivity and profits.

Having a policy in place that defines organisation values and clarifies behaviour expectations may be the first step towards a more emotionally intelligent approach, but influencing people's attitudes and dealing effectively with unacceptable behaviour may require a fundamental culture shift. Management at every level have a key responsibility for ensuring employees' behaviour matches expected standards.

Along with this responsibility, it is crucially important that managers are exemplars in building and maintaining productive working relationships based on mutual respect.

EQ in Practice

There's always a danger of focusing on the negative because of its heightened potential for dramatic headlines. Announcing a disaster, or reporting on how things have gone wrong, generally has the capability to invoke more drama and interest than a *'positive news'* story. (Remember the *'good news'* publication that was founded and failed – their last issue headline being *'No war declared in 16 weeks!'* – not exactly riveting stuff to attract readers' interest.)

But now for the good news! There are a number of organisations out there where people show what emotional intelligence means in practice. And lessons learnt are just as valid and valuable as those from more dramatic negative examples. It's the same principle as learning from any aspect of good practice. For while headlines rightly tend to emphasise a need for analysis and changes in practice when things go wrong, examining why and how things have gone well provides equally powerful learning opportunities.

Brief examples of EQ practice include:

- The comedy writer and film director Richard Curtis who wrote a New Year episode of the *'Vicar of Dibley'*, with a story specifically designed to move people to compassion for the poor. By chance, the episode was broadcast shortly after the tragic news of the Boxing Day 2004 Asian tsunami, and helped to draw people's attention to the plight of the thousands of poor survivors. (Richard Curtis's article in the Sunday Times, News Review January 9th 2005 provides a moving account of his own tsunami experience and his work for the *'Make Poverty History'* campaign.)

- The work programmes organised by the charity Betel, that helps drug users overcome their addiction and develop self-respect and emotional stability.

- The Crown Prosecution Service's pioneering programme that draws on emotional intelligence to help lawyers' understanding of the emotions experienced by victims of serious crimes. (Reported in *People Management*, August 2002.)

These three brief examples all illustrate an understanding of emotions, and a heightened consciousness of the importance of recognising their impact. The police chief who, in an effort to influence people to talk to each other, banned staff from sending e-mails (other than those deemed strictly necessary) on one day each week, is a further example of a leader striving to influence people's emotional connection. (Roger Baker, Chief Constable, Essex Constabulary, reported in the Daily Mail, 6th August 2005.)

The following stories of emotional connection include the influence exerted by Professor Sumantra Ghoshal in his role as adviser to global companies, and the story of how library staff at Sighthill Library in Edinburgh engaged a group of disaffected (and badly behaved) teenagers through using an emotionally intelligent approach.

The Transnational Corporation

The *'Transnational Corporation'* was the brain child of the late management theorist Professor Sumantra Ghoshal, the founding Dean of the Indian School of Business in Hyderabad, and Christopher Bartlett, Professor at Harvard Graduate School of Business Administration. The book they co-authored, *Managing Across Borders: The Transnational Solution*, has been listed in the Financial Times as one of the 50 most influential management books and translated into nine languages.

Sumantra Ghoshal was recognised for his research, teaching and consultancy on strategic, organisational and managerial issues confronting global companies. He authored or co-authored a total of 12 books, and had over 70 articles and several award-winning case studies published.

As an outspoken critic of bureaucracy, in *The Individualised Corporation* he argued that businesses should follow the examples of companies such as ABB (formerly Asea Brown Boveri, a multinational corporation based in Switzerland specialising in power and automation technologies) and General Electric (voted as the *'world's most admired company'*) and reconfigure themselves to fit around the talents and abilities of the people who work for them. A central theme in the book was that organisation change is best effected by infusing every member of a business with a sense of common purpose. His advocated approach was to manage companies in ways that trusted in people's best intentions and assumed their good faith rather than their mean-spiritedness.

And on a personal level, his style was to find a positive result to every dilemma. He was known for always trying to support other people's ideas, and he also had the reputation of refusing to tolerate mediocrity, whilst being quick to spot and reward talent.

EQ key message: Encourage people to achieve their potential - and trust in their best intentions.

Emotional intelligence was apparent at the forefront of Sumantra Ghoshal's behaviour in the personal approach he used to communicate with people, through listening, seeking to understand them and by acknowledging their ideas. His emphasis on a management approach that infused a sense of common purpose, trusted people and their good intentions, and sought best fit between people's talents and abilities (rather than building bureaucratic organisational processes that stifle these), championed EQ practice and its influence at a strategic level.

To engage effectively with people we need to communication with openness, honesty and trust. And trust is a bit like love – the more you give the more you tend to get. (Not always true I know – but as a general principle it works on an emotional level.) The question is really whether you find yourself at the end of two extremes, either finding it difficult to trust people and being consistently suspicious about their intentions, or conversely, trusting too easily to the extent of being gullible and not looking after your own interests.

Being disposed to trust and developing a deeper sense of trust through emotionally engaging with others and seeking to

---

build effective relationships is the EQ approach. Taking a genuine interest in, showing respect for and valuing others, and balancing this with self respect, openness and honesty is the emotionally intelligent way. (For more about self/other balance, see *'Assertiveness'* in the chapter on *'Developing Emotional Competence'*.)

Engaging with young people

> *'Communication depends on our ability to make sense of the world as we perceive it and to understand the perceived world as others describe it.'*
>
> Geoff Cox
> (Experiential learning designer)

Most of us can remember from our schooldays that it was not necessarily the subject of study that engaged our attention, but the teacher's passion for the topic combined with their interest in us as individuals that inspired our attentiveness and engaged our motivation. A positive example of applied EQ in the public sector is the inspiring story of Evelyn Kilmurray, the senior library officer and other staff at Sighthill Library in Edinburgh. How they dealt with a group of young people who were behaving badly is reminiscent of the approach used by teachers and others to inspire a motivation to achieve – that is, by listening to people and seeking to engage with them on an emotional level, and then doing something practical that maintains interest and creates self-motivation.

Sighthill Library in Edinburgh is located in a community of

deprivation with an unemployment rate of 18%. Within the area, the library was often the only public facility open, which meant that a lot of unaccompanied young people tended to use it. And in 2004, the behaviour of some of these young people was not only becoming more antisocial, and upsetting for both staff and other library visitors, it was also becoming more difficult to deal with.

The staff approach had previously been to ban the troublemakers from the building. But instead of solving the problem, the young people concerned just hung around the front door and created even more trouble! So, how did the situation change in a few short months, from having consistent problems with young people's antisocial behaviour to not only having no bad behaviour incidents, but influencing former troublemakers to become motivated to learn and achieve?

The first step was employing more young people as library staff who had a less traditional approach to librarianship, led by Evelyn Kilmurray, the senior library officer. Instead of banning them (which clearly didn't work in any case), staff began to engage with the young troublemakers by asking what they wanted from the library service – and then tried to work with them and with other organisations to provide what they were looking for. (If any bad behaviour started up again, rather than being banned, the culprits were sent outside for 15 minutes to calm down, and then allowed to return.)

As a result, schemes such as the Duke of Edinburgh Award, new courses including dance groups, drama workshops and a football-based literacy programme were some of the new offerings developed in partnership with other organisations. A gamers' workshop, where people learnt how to develop their own computer games was an initiative of particular appeal to young people that inspired their interest and subsequently their good behaviour.

The benefits that resulted were not only a more effective library service with a wider range of activities that was pleasant to visit and fully utilised, but it also inspired a number of the former troublemakers who had previously been disengaged with education, to be motivated to go to study at college. So it was a simple approach that started with genuinely attempting to understand the underlying causes of the bad behaviour, by respecting, listening to and engaging with people, that began a gradual process of positive behaviour change from the young people concerned.

EQ key message - communicate, listen and engage

It's so easy for us to condemn others when we encounter inappropriate behaviour without first seeking to understand what experience and emotions may lie beneath this. Making a genuine attempt to view the world from another's perspective is an emotionally intelligent way to behave. And taking what may seem a brave step outside a normal comfort zone can not only pay dividends in self-worth (valuing your attribute of dealing assertively rather than aggressively with a tricky situation), but also raise the perpetrators' self-esteem because they feel valued and listened to. For when people feel valued and listened to (especially where this may not have been a significant part of their previous experience), they are more likely to not only have increased self-esteem, but also to give more consideration to their behaviour towards others.

While the actions of Evelyn Kilmurray and other library staff may have initially been perceived as ill-judged or foolhardy, the benefits were not only to the young people themselves and the library users and staff, but also to the local community – and ultimately to wider society.

The EQ message is not to instantly condemn others, but to genuinely listen to and strive to understand others' concerns, issues and priorities and the emotions associated with these. Focusing on *behaviour* rather than the person is also a useful EQ reminder. The EQ approach is to develop a mindset that, when dealing with others' inappropriate behaviour, avoids instant reactions, and strives instead to respond in a more considered, reflective way that takes account of the overall context and the emotions involved.

7

Developing Emotional Competence

> '*It's what you learn after you know it all that counts.*'
>
> John Wooden
> (American basketball coach – and the only athlete to be honoured in the basketball Hall of Fame as both player and coach)

Introduction

So, now to the really important bit: how to put emotional intelligence into practice – that is, have EQ at the forefront of your thinking in dealing with your own and others' emotions in the rollercoaster ride of human interactions.

The diversity of human emotions, their scope, intensity and complexity and the circumstances in which they're experienced, mean that putting EQ into practice can be a significant personal challenge. The challenge starts with your commitment to be more emotionally intelligent. This requires heightened self-awareness, a profound and conscious recognition of the impact of your behaviour on others, an openness to learn and change, and a generous dose of self-esteem. The only way to develop and maintain emotional intelligence is through intensified and focused awareness both of self and of others, and through reflective practice built on a foundation of continuing learning and change. So it's a journey rather than a destination, and definitely not a '*quick fix*'.

This chapter consists of nine sections. Three of these provide overall frameworks (*The EQ4U Process, Emotional Engagement* and *Effective Communication*); three relate to specific attributes of emotional intelligence and the behaviours associated with these (*Receiving and Giving Constructive Feedback, Empathetic Listening* and *Assertiveness*); one focuses specifically on contributing to the development of effective teamwork (*Developing 'Team Engagement Rules'*); one (*Renewal Balance*) is an exercise for reflection on maintaining renewal within 4 key areas; and the final section (*Emotional Sagacity – the EQ Checklist*) is designed as a quick and easy EQ reference reminder.

Brief explanations of each section as follows:

• The EQ4U Process

A core understanding of the thinking sequence is needed as the foundation to becoming more emotionally intelligent – hence the starting point for developing emotional competence. The EQ4U process was originally introduced in the book, *Mindchange – The Power of Emotionally Intelligent Leadership* (2005).

• Emotional Engagement

This section provides a core framework for developing and maintaining productive and meaningful relationships with the people in your life.

• Receiving and Giving Constructive Feedback

Being able to receive and give constructive feedback is an essential attribute of being emotionally intelligent, and merits a section of its own.

• Empathetic Listening

Empathetic listening is a fundamental attribute that underpins emotional competence. Empathetic listening differs significantly from *'listening to respond'* (which tends to be a frequently used *'listening'* approach!). It moves on from what is described as *'active listening'* and the behavioural techniques involved, to an approach that strives for real engagement and empathy with others.

- **Assertiveness**

Assertiveness is thought by many people to focus entirely on being self-confident and positive, along with an ability to state own views in a forthright way. However, while assertiveness is certainly about being confident and positive, it is also about respect for others and achieving an appropriate balance between one's own and others' needs. Its meaning, as understood in personal development terms, encompasses both self-esteem and respect for others. Assertiveness is included as an element of *'Developing Emotional Competence'*, because of the association between behaviours recognised as being both assertive and emotionally competent.

- **Developing 'Team Engagement Rules'**

'Team Engagement Rules' are the behavioural ground rules for working as a team. This element includes an outline of the principles behind the rules and examples of what these might include.

- **Effective Communication**

Effective communication is based on the 4 key elements of context, clarity, genuineness and warmth. The *'Communication Checklist'* included in this section outlines how these elements relate to good communication practice, and how information, ideas and feelings can be imparted or exchanged in emotionally intelligent ways.

- **Renewal Balance**

This is about reflection and reflective practice relating to purpose, intellectual, physical and emotional dimensions of our lives; important in contributing to *maintaining* emotional competence.

- **Emotional Sagacity – the EQ Checklist**

The section concludes with an easy-reference checklist of sagacious EQ characteristics and behaviours which show emotional wisdom and good judgement.

The EQ4U Process

EQ4U describes the steps to emotional intelligence, using a *'traffic lights'* three-phase metaphor to provide an easy-to-remember way of conscious EQ application. The EQ4U process is a reminder to focus first on a heightened awareness of both your own and others' emotions, and then comprehensively reflect on how to deal with these, before taking action.

●	**STOP**	Check your own and others' values and emotions, and their expression
●	**REFLECT**	Make sense of these values and emotions, and how they interact
●	**ACTION**	Use emotionally intelligent behaviour, and communicate appropriately to others

Step 1: Self-awareness and understanding

Step 1 is about being prepared to listen to, and reflect on, your intuitive feelings. What do you really feel about the issue you are facing or the problem you are dealing with? This doesn't mean ignoring objective facts or collecting information to help you make better decisions; it just means taking account of the feelings that you have as well.

More conscious awareness of your inner body language 'signals' and associated emotions helps to check whether you may have feelings that you are trying to suppress. Awareness of the signals you are giving to others by your outward body language is also important in self-awareness; could this be giving away indicators to others about what you are thinking and feeling without being aware of it yourself? Improving your self-awareness is the first step to raising your EQ.

You must know yourself, and understand the way that your own feelings are working, before you can get to grips with the way that you interact emotionally with others.

Step 2: Awareness and understanding of others

Step 2 is being interested in other people, in what they are thinking and feeling, and being aware of their body language and behaviours. How do people react to you? Do they look you in the eye? Do they seem pleased if you take an interest in what they are doing? Do they relax when you are present? Or do they avoid direct eye contact, tense up and look worried when you appear?

The range of physical expressions that people make as a result of different emotions can have subtle but meaningful differences. To be more emotionally aware, you need to be able to anticipate and interpret these by taking account of the situation you and they are in, and observe what people do and how they do it. Recognising others' emotions, understanding what is generating them and anticipating how and when they may occur is a key element of the EQ process. With foresight, you can anticipate when negative emotions are likely to happen to others and reflect on what these might signify to them. So the first two EQ4U stages are described as the *'red light phase'* because of the importance of stopping to focus on both your own and others' emotional reactions and give careful consideration to their meaning.

Step 3: Reflection

This third step of EQ4U takes us into the *'amber phase'* (the second traffic light), the time for focused reflection – in other words, still maintaining caution by being circumspect about emotional meaning, and reflecting on an appropriate way to respond. Reflective response means maintaining careful thought that strives to make sense of values and emotions and how they interact – rather than going for instant reactions.

Understanding the ethical framework of principles and values that shape your judgements and decisions is fundamental to emotional intelligence. Reflection starts with looking in at yourself and asking searching questions about why you do things the way you do and what values and principles really guide your life. As well as looking in on yourself (emotionally intelligent behaviour can be described as an *'inside out'* approach), it's also about reflecting on the external situation, including your own and others' circumstances. What has caused this situation to arise? Why has it happened here, now? Reflection involves looking beyond the immediate situation to consider the past and its effect on the present.

From that you can then reflect on your own emotions and what impact you anticipate others' emotions are likely to have. Our emotions are a product of more than the moment; they are the result of a complex series of interacting experiences that have conditioned us to react in a particular way. Two people who were once friends but have had a falling out will react very differently to an experience. When they were friends it might have been laughed at, while now it may well cause anger and resentment. Understanding what may shape their emotional reaction, and yours, is fundamental to the EQ process.

Emotionally aware people reflect on how they communicate with others – to think before they speak. They choose words that show that they recognise and understand the context, so that their words are perceived as being appropriate to the situation, and they are clear in what they say. And they always strive to be genuine, open and honest. But that's only possible if they reflect carefully about what they really think and believe, and if it fits with their value and belief system.

Finally, they ensure that their communication demonstrates an appropriate degree of warmth. What are they trying to communicate through their words? It's not just what they say but how they say it that counts. They reflect on the tone of their voice, their posture, their proximity to the people they are speaking to and their other body language, to make sure that they are being authentic and communicating the same message as their words.

The more open you are to yourself about how you feel, the easier it is to be open to others. Revealing your doubts and uncertainties is not a sign of weakness, although far too many people think it is. It only becomes a weakness if it holds you back from acting. Making decisions on partial or conflicting information often means that you will have doubts about the validity of your decisions. However, should you reveal those doubts, then you should make your decision and be prepared to carry it through. The critical thing is to distinguish between the uncertainties that lie behind the decisions and the conviction with which you carry out the course of action you have determined.

Step 4: Application

The final phase of the EQ4U process is action. After careful reflection now you have the *'green light'* to move forward. Being aware of, and reflecting on, the meaning of your own and others' emotional states must lead to *action* if you want to be more emotionally competent – action that is informed by these insights into your own and others' emotions and feelings, attitudes, values and beliefs – and action that is informed by analysis of the situation and by consideration of the options. EQ4U is not only about only reacting with emotional awareness; it is about matching rational analysis with emotional analysis so that you are more fully aware.

To demonstrate emotional competence you must respond to others with behaviour that reflects both your own emotions and their emotional state, and matches the ethical principles and values that you regard as important. You must communicate genuinely, openly and honestly. Developing your EQ is not quick, but that doesn't mean it's difficult, just demanding. Demanding because you have to be able to be brutally honest with yourself if you want to be honest to others, and because when you look deeply into yourself, your feelings and your values, you may not always like what you see.

It is often the case that those who may be most in need of emotional intelligence development recognise the need for it the least! Any suggestion that they would benefit from personal development is therefore generally met with denial, defensiveness and sometimes downright aggression. Defensiveness and aggression often however mask an inner lack of confidence – whereas confident, self-assured people are often also the most self-effacing and the most open to learn.

A range of behaviours involved in the EQ4U process are covered in the following sections. What is important to remember, however, is that while the *'traffic lights'* model is intended as a simple metaphor to emphasise thought before action, the process itself is frequently complex. A more complete model of EQ4U is therefore as follows:

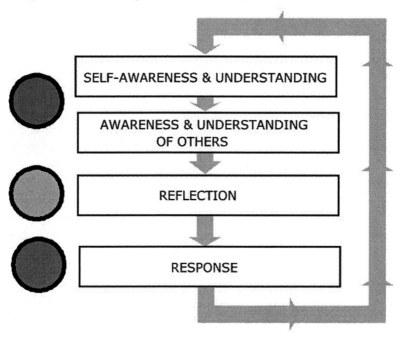

Emotional Engagement

> Emotional engagement means developing affinity with others by connecting with them in a principled and authentic way that establishes a genuine interest in and concern for their wellbeing.

Making emotional connections with others and building trusted and valued relationships is achieved through demonstrating emotionally intelligent behaviour based on a foundation of key personal characteristics. If you are striving to achieve trusted and valued relationships, the question you need to ask yourself is: *How do I make a positive emotional connection with this individual/group in my communication with them either directly or indirectly?* The following checklist may be useful:

Acknowledging emotions
- Acknowledge and understand others' emotions and priorities within the situational context by *'holistic'* and attentive listening, – i.e. not only hearing the words they say but also being tuned into their expression through both overt and subtle body language indicators.

Understanding and empathising
- Understand and empathise with others' vulnerabilities, limitations and concerns – by acknowledging their views and how these are communicated, and without diminishing or dismissing their expression.

Managing own emotions

- Manage your own emotions – by acknowledging, understanding and dealing with them effectively through being sensitive to their expression and emotional impact on others (for instance, being angry without losing your temper and upset without being dramatic), and strive to be in the motivational state* most appropriate to the situation.

  (*Refer to www.apterinternational.com for further information on motivational states/Reversal Theory. *'The Myths of Motivation'* and *'Improving organisation performance – Reversal Theory and Work'* can also be found on: http://www.eq4u.co.uk/eq_review.htm.)

Sharing vulnerabilities

- Share your own vulnerabilities – by showing your human side and your own limitations and doing this in a self-effacing way appropriate to the situation.

Being authentic

- Be authentic – by being genuine, open and honest in your communication and expression, and by having *'authentic presence'*, i.e. matching what you say with what you do, and standing by your principles despite setbacks or opposition.

Keeping commitments

- Keep commitments – by consistently keeping your word, or if this is not possible for some reason, explaining honestly and fully why promises have not been met.

Showing interest and concern

- Show interest in, and concern for, others at a personal level (remembering the *'little things'*) – by being generally kind and considerate and by acknowledging situations that may be important to them. (Examples include saying *'thank you'* when a job is well done, remembering and acknowledging birthdays, accomplishments and other details about their personal circumstances.)

Acknowledging others

* Acknowledge others' communication – by responding in a timely way with genuineness, clarity of message and context, and with an appropriate degree of warmth.

'Emotional Engagement' is available as a PDF download via the EQ Review section of the EQ Learning Resources website: http://www.eq4u.co.uk/eq_review.htm.

Receiving and Giving Constructive Feedback

> *'The trouble with most of us is that we would rather be ruined by praise that saved by criticism.'*
>
> Norman Vincent Peale,
> (American cleric, and author of *The Power of Positive Thinking,* first published in 1952)

Being able to receive and give constructive feedback is an important attribute of being emotional intelligent. And seeking out feedback to learn how to be more effective can be a positive learning tool. Ensure however that you are prepared to listen and learn from the negative, rather than just seek out the positive.

An essential element of self-development is having the willingness and ability to receive and give feedback in a way that is non-offensive to either party, and provides the opportunity to learn and change. So when you are the recipient of feedback (*both positive and negative*), if you perceive this as a *'gift'* and remember that it offers the possibility of learning how to improve and grow in effectiveness then you are more likely to appreciate and welcome it.

When feedback is given constructively you are more likely to respond in a positive way. Should you receive non-constructive feedback, you will find that a response focusing on facts and objectivity rather than on a defensive or aggressive reaction is likely to result in a more productive outcome. Similar *'engagement rules'* therefore apply to *receiving* feedback as to giving feedback, i.e. focusing on *facts* and *objectivity*. Focusing on facts helps you to learn from both praise and criticism, and to respond to negative feedback helpfully rather than destructively.

Before you are able to *give* feedback constructively, you need first to be able to *receive* it constructively. The following *'engagement rules'* will help you to maximise your feedback learning:

Receiving Feedback Constructively

• Be objective
You are likely to receive feedback more constructively when you are in a relatively unemotional state. Emotions such as happiness, anger, etc., can amplify and distort the message. To receive feedback constructively, strive therefore to maintain a state where strong emotions are not aroused.

• Don't be defensive
Stay calm and accept anything said to you that is factually based. Respond objectively rather than defensively.

• Don't make assumptions
Use appropriate questions to check facts rather than support assumptions. Summarise to check your understanding of the point being made.

• Focus on facts
Ask for behaviour examples if the feedback you get is vague or judgemental.

• Listen
Don't interrupt. Ask questions to clarify.

• Avoid external attribution
Try to avoid the common response of attributing positive feedback to yourself, and negative feedback to the situation (*'It was only a simulation'*) or to others (*'It was the group I was working with'*) – but accept praise graciously that is genuinely given!

• Use appropriate body language
Ensure your body language matches what you are saying and that you are genuine in your response.

• Decide for yourself
Allow yourself reflection time to consider the feedback carefully, and make your own decision about whether to believe it and whether or

not to modify your behaviour as a result of the feedback. Accept, in any case, that feedback given can inform you about the impression you give to others, and can therefore be perceived seen as a *'gift'*.

• Do not overcompensate
Do not overcompensate as a result of negative feedback. If you wish to modify your behaviour, make moderate changes and then evaluate the outcomes.

Giving Feedback Constructively

• Consider what your objectives are for giving feedback
Ensure your intention is to be helpful rather than destructive if you are planning to criticise. Constructive feedback is supportive feedback, given with a positive purpose and not with the intent to be damaging or destructive towards the recipient.

• Be objective
In common with receiving feedback, when giving feedback you are also likely to be more effective when you are in a relatively unemotional state, since any emotions which you are feeling can amplify and distort the message.

• Be specific and descriptive
Identify specifically what you are giving feedback on, and describe this appropriately.

• Focus on what you see, not what you believe – don't make assumptions!
Focus on evidence of what you've actually seen or heard, ensuring you don't express opinions as facts, and use appropriate questions to check facts rather than make assumptions before making judgements.

• Concentrate on behaviour nor personality
Express what was said or done by the other person(s) to support your feedback, rather than make personality judgements.

- **Separate description from evaluation**

After describing the behaviour, state its impact on you, how it is perceived by you, and how you feel about it (*and how it may have been perceived by others if this is appropriate*).

- **Use feedback to inform, not to advise**

Offer suggestions as to what others might do differently, rather than direct them to do what you think they ought to do. When you think a change of behaviour would be appropriate, use expressions like *'You could consider...'*, or *'There are alternative options/approaches'*, rather than being directive with: *'You should...'*, *'You must...'*, *'You ought...'*, etc.

- **Respect individual differences**

Acknowledge the other person's right to be different, and respect their right to have a point of view that's different to yours.

- **Focus on what can be changed and not on what can't**

When criticising others, tell them about things you feel need to be changed which they are *able* to change. For example, social behaviour can be altered whereas intellectual attributes probably cannot.

- **Balance positive and negative**

Ensure that not all of your feedback is critical. Use opportunities to tell others what you like about their behaviour rather than just looking for their faults.

- **Use appropriate body language**

Ensure your body language matches what you are saying and that you are being authentic in your approach.

Effective Praise

When considering feedback skills, it is often forgotten that effective praise also plays an important part in giving productive feedback to others. A frequent comment about managers is that they tend to focus on the things that are wrong (and often give destructive criticism!), but tend not to praise when things are going well.

Praising people, if carried out authentically is a behaviour which is generally welcome and tends to encourage people to do well. Effective praise lets the person know that you have noted what they have done, and that you value their achievements. Paying genuine and meaningful tributes to people's accomplishments in a timely way and, in the appropriate place, is praise well given.

The following two sections contrast less effective and more effective ways of giving praise, and help to serve as a reminder that giving constructive praise can be just as valuable as providing supportive criticism.

Less Effective Praise

• Generalised comments
Dishing out general comments, such as 'You're doing a good job', with no further explanation as to why behaviour is being commended can be meaningless, and it often rolls off the back of the person who receives it.

There are two key dangers with giving generalised comments. The first is that while the intention may be genuine, the recipient may not understand what you mean by it. The second is the danger that such a comment can come over as being patronising, even suggesting that you disparage the person being praised by assuming they will be encouraged just because you've said something! This is especially relevant to those who are already highly motivated and may see the intention as trying to provide unnecessary additional motivation.

• Praise for expected performance
While praise for expected performance may be of value in some circumstances – for example, if the recipient seems to be feeling 'down' and you feel that a positive comment may make them feel better – what is often the case is that if praise is given for an assumed standard of performance, there is the danger that this can come over as condescending or sarcastic. Or, or at the very least, the recipient

might wonder why they are being praised. (If someone is feeling down, empathetic listening is in any case more likely to be an appropriate approach.)

• The 'sandwich' system

Productive working and personal relationships usually develop better when people are straight with each other. Praise, when deserved, and given genuinely, is believable; when mixed with criticism, it is suspect. Praise given as a precursor to criticism, with the real intention of making the person more receptive to the criticism to follow, is not effective feedback. Following with another item of praise for the same purpose, completes the 'sandwich'.

So when praise is in order, give it warmly; and when criticism is appropriate, convey it constructively and in a supportive way. This is more effective and authentic, rather than mixing the two in a deliberate attempt to try and make someone receptive.

• Praise handed out lavishly in front of others

Congratulations, tributes or compliments that are only given when more senior people are present does not come over as honest and well-meaning. Saving praise for such occasions can give the impression (whether accurate or not) that the intention is to impress rather than to give authentic praise.

More Effective Praise

• Specific praise

Always follow a general comment with a specific example. For example, after starting with, *'You did a great job dealing with that customer who had a difficult query this afternoon'*, continue with, *'I think you handled it well because despite his obvious wish to seek a quick solution, you listened attentively, and asked the right questions to make sure you had all the relevant facts before suggesting an answer.'*

Specific feedback communicates to the person that you really noticed, and that what you observed or heard deserves praise. Praise of this kind demonstrates that you were aware of and valued the way things were done, and can give useful feedback to the person concerned.

• Praise for better than expected results

The obvious times to give praise are for better-than-expected results – for example, for exceeding a target or for making an extra special effort that goes beyond what would normally be expected. But when people make a special effort to achieve performance excellence and it is consistently either overlooked or ignored, they're unlikely to be motivated to continually strive to achieve outstanding results.

So noticing and seeking opportunities to pay tribute to people's achievements, and conveying this constructively is the route to effective praise. And giving praise constructively by recognising and seeking to inspire others' positive emotions is being emotionally intelligent.

Empathetic Listening

From:
'Walk a mile in my shoes' by Joe South

If I could be you and you could be me for just one hour
If we could find a way to get inside each other's mind
If you could see you through my eyes instead of your own ego
I believe you'd be surprised to see that you'd been blind

Walk a mile in my shoes, walk a mile in my shoes
Before you abuse, criticise and accuse
Walk a mile in my shoes......

Introduction

Empathy can be described as having the capacity to relate to others on an emotional level, to such an extent that you can imagine the same sensation as those who are actually experiencing it. Words associated with its meaning include: compassion, caring, understanding, consideration, commiseration, feeling, sensitivity, awareness, sympathy and rapport. Because feelings and emotions are intensely personal, we can never truly *'know'* how someone else feels. Empathy is the closest we can come to understanding and connecting with others at an emotional level.

A key part of being empathetic means being a good listener; and empathetic listening is the pinnacle of listening engagement. It differs significantly from simply hearing what someone is saying, and responding without having engaged with the person.

Empathetic listening is also a fundamental attribute of being emotionally intelligent and underpins EQ approach and behaviour. And in emotional intelligence terms, empathetic listening means listening to yourself as well as others, and taking notice of your *'inner voice'* and the psychological and physical messages your mind and body are giving to you.

Barriers that prevent effective listening include: external distractions (such as noise or other environmental factors); internal distractions (such as daydreaming, being pre-occupied with other thoughts – or perhaps having a headache or being hungry); mentally formulating a counter-argument whilst the person is still speaking; or simply a lack of interest in the subject or the person. Behaviours that indicate you are not listening include: interrupting; talking over; avoiding eye contact – and ignoring obvious body language *'signals'* (such as those associated with anger or anxiety).

Empathetic Listening 'Engagement Rules'

To be an effective and empathetic listener, the following *'Engagement Rules'* apply:

• Limit your own talking
Concentrate on the other person – and remember to focus on listening to understand, rather than thinking about your response.

• Recognise the other person's point of view
Acknowledge their right to their point of view and their associated feelings and emotions – and don't say, *'I know how you feel.'* (*You don't!*)

• Ask questions
Check your understanding by asking appropriate questions – use open rather than leading questions. Clarify if you seem to be getting contradictory messages.

• Don't interrupt
Allow the speaker to finish (and don't finish off their sentences!).

• Concentrate
Focus on what is being said – shut out distractions.

- ## Take notes
While in most circumstances these will be mental notes, in some instances (e.g. if the listening is part of a business discussion) it may be appropriate to make written notes to help remember important points – but be selective.

- ## Listen for ideas – not just words
Use your judgement to analyse messages – but make sure you're not making assumptions.

- ## Reflect back
To demonstrate you've listened and understood, summarise what's been said in your own words, but ensure you do this selectively and at the appropriate time.

- ## Respond to ideas rather than the person
Remain objective and don't take things personally – focus on facts.

- ## Be aware of both body language and tone of voice
Recognise and seek to understand both your own and the other person's body language and tone of voice and the messages conveyed in this. And ensure your body language and tone convey appropriate signals.

- ## Maintain silence as appropriate
Be sensitive to times during a discussion when maintaining silence is the right thing to do – without feeling pressure to fill any *'silence gaps'*.

- ## Truly engage
And most of all, strive to truly engage with the person by being genuinely interested in what they are seeking to convey and by seeking understanding of the meaning behind their words (or their silence) and the emotions they may be experiencing.

> *'If I cannot understand my friend's silence, I will never get to understand his words.'*
>
> Enoch Powell
> (Late UK Conservative politician)

Assertiveness

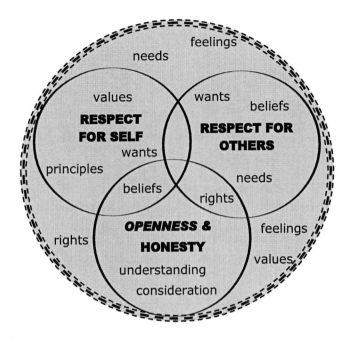

Being assertive is balancing the three elements of *a)* respect for self, and *b)* respect for others, with *c)* openness and honesty. It means demonstrating understanding of, and equal consideration for, both your own and others' needs, wants, feelings, rights and beliefs.

The principle that underpins an assertive approach and behaviour is that your needs or wants are as important as other people's and should therefore be treated with equal consideration. The alternatives are to believe that your needs or wants are either *more* or *less* important than those of others.

Seeing yourself as deserving more respect than others can result in an aggressive approach and self-important behaviour. Conversely, seeing yourself as deserving less respect than others can result in a submissive approach and self-deprecating behaviour. Assertiveness is therefore about having a positive image of both self and others, and behaving in a way that reinforces mutual respect.

To clarify the differences between each approach, the following sections outline the distinctions between aggressive, submissive and assertive behaviours. This is followed by an overview of the *'3 Steps to Assertiveness'* approach.

Aggressive behaviour

> *'Never look down on someone unless you are helping them up.'*
>
> Reverend Jesse Jackson
> (American civil rights leader and politician)

Aggressive behaviour is based on the belief that you and your rights, wants, needs, feelings, opinions, etc., are more important than other people's, and is clearly not conducive to building productive working or personal relationships It is often characterised by accusing and blaming other people, showing contempt, and being hostile or patronising.

Aggressive behaviour is indicated by:

* Standing up for your rights in such a way that you violate the rights of another person.
* Expressing your thoughts, feelings and beliefs in unsuitable and inappropriate ways – even though you may honestly believe those views to be right.
* Making excessive use of *'I'* statements.
* Stating opinion as facts.
* Using threats.
* Putting others down.
* Making a lot of use of the words *'ought'*, *'must'*, *'should'* and *'have to'*.
* Being keen to attach blame to others.
* Using either open or subtle sarcasm to make a point or to put others down.

Aggressive behaviour falls into two distinct categories: overt and covert aggression. Overt aggression is behaviour that openly indicates to others a belief that your rights, wants and needs are more important than theirs. On the other hand, covertly aggressive behaviour (which still holds the higher self-importance belief) is more subtle in its approach. Overt aggression includes behaviours such as raised tone of voice, obvious put-downs and open threats; covert aggression includes a sarcastic tone of voice, insinuated put-downs and subtly implied threats.

Submissive behaviour

> *'I've never had a humble opinion. If you've got an opinion, why be humble about it?'*
>
> Joan Baez
> (Song writer and folk singer)

Conversely, submissive behaviour is based on the belief that your rights, wants, needs, feelings, opinions, etc., are relatively unimportant compared to others. Typical of submissive behaviour traits are long, justifying, self-deprecating explanations and ingratiating attempts to accommodate the needs and wants of other people.

Submissive behaviour is indicated by:

- Failing to stand up for your rights, or doing so in such a way that others can easily disregard them.
- Expressing your thoughts, feelings and beliefs in apologetic, cautious or self-deprecating ways.
- Failing to express your views or feelings altogether.
- Making long, rambling (often justifying) statements.
- Avoiding making *'I'* statements, or qualifying them, e.g. *'It's only my opinion but...'*

While submissive behaviour may be appropriate in some circumstances, whether or not it is emotionally intelligent depends on whether you have consciously and freely chosen to allow another person's needs to take precedence over yours (such as choosing to give in to a loved one's preference when this is likely to help towards a better long-term relationship!)

Assertive behaviour

> *'Real maturity is the ability to imagine the humanity of every person as fully as you believe in your own humanity.'*
>
> Tobias Wolff
> (Author of *This Boy's Life*)

There is a clear distinction between the meanings of the terms *'assertiveness'* and *'emotional intelligence'*. However, because assertiveness is based on high self-esteem, treating others with equal respect and openness and honesty, there is significant alignment between assertive and emotionally intelligent behaviour.

Assertive behaviour is indicated by:

- Mutual respect – that is, respecting yourself and expecting others to respect you, and treating others with equal respect as human beings regardless of their individual position in society or in a hierarchy.

- Standing up for your legitimate rights – by an honest, open and direct expression of your point of view, which at the same time shows that you respect the other person's point of view and are not seeking to violate their rights.

- Recognising others' equal right to be assertive – and encouraging them to be assertive when their behaviour is either submissive or aggressive.

- Recognising a responsibility towards others – rather than being responsible for others. And deciding whether or not to be responsible for finding a solution to someone else's problem. (Distinguishing the difference between having responsibility towards each other as adults and our responsibility as adults for and towards our children and those who may be in our care)

- Taking personal responsibility – for your own behaviour and response to others, regardless of the inappropriateness of their behaviour.

- Recognising your own needs and wants independently of others – that is, understanding and communicating these appropriately and clearly, without seeking general approval.

- Expressing needs and wants – in a confident way (rather than hoping someone will notice, or dropping hints, and then complaining later that you didn't get what you needed or wanted!)

- Expressing feelings, beliefs and opinions in ways which are direct, honest and appropriate – carefully and clearly stating own views about thoughts and feelings without apologising for them! (i.e. not saying 'I'm sorry but I think.....'!) And remembering that while some things you say can be refuted, your feelings and emotions can't.

- Saying 'sorry' when appropriate – i.e. apologising sincerely when you recognise your behaviour has been out of order or when you have made a mistake (without justifying or being defensive!); and saying 'I'm sorry' to express genuine sympathy towards others. (A typical example of a use of the word 'sorry' which is *not* strictly appropriate is when someone says 'Excuse me' because they want you to move out of their way, and you apologise and move. An apologetic 'Sorry' would be appropriate if you're deliberately blocking their way, but if this isn't the case then a simple 'Certainly' or 'Of course' or a similarly friendly response would be more assertive – or just politely moving out of the way!)

- Allowing for mistakes – that is, recognising that it is OK to make a mistake (providing this is done with good intentions); and recognising that what is important is how a mistake is handled and what is learnt from the experience.

- Setting clear boundaries – i.e. clarifying to others in a straight-forward and appropriate way what is and isn't acceptable.

- Distinguishing between fact and opinion – making it clear in your communication whether you are expressing fact or opinion.

- Using open-ended questions – to genuinely seek the thoughts and opinions and needs of others.

Assertiveness is also about:

- Genuinely seeking ways to resolve problems.

- Making statements that are brief and to the point.

- Using 'I' statements (but not excessively!).

- Asking for 'thinking it over' time when this is appropriate.

The '3 Steps to Assertiveness'

The following is described as the *'three steps'* approach to assertiveness, and is useful as a behaviour sequence guideline. It is appropriate in a range of situations, and especially when you are in disagreement with someone who is forcefully expressing their views; or in circumstances when you want to assert yourself because you think something has been said that is inappropriate or offensive in some way to you or others.

What is important in using this approach is a genuine underpinning respect for the other person and a wish to reach a positive outcome. What is not appropriate – and definitely not emotionally intelligent, is using the *'3 steps'* as an *'assertive technique'* without being authentic.

STEP 1 – listening and understanding, and saying something to demonstrate this

Step 1, engaging with the other person and genuinely listening to what they have to say, is the one that is most often missed out when assertiveness is first being practised. Step 1 is important whether you agree with what has been said or not. Even if your view is totally in opposition with what the other person is saying, it shows you have sincerely listened and understood, and that you respect their right to their opinion. This crucial first step of genuinely listening to the other person not only indicates your consideration for the other person's viewpoint, it also allows you brief but valuable thinking time for your response in steps two and three.

So, first engage with the other person, and demonstrate your authentic consideration of them, by focusing on them and empathetically listening to what is being said. And if you haven't fully comprehended what they've said, check your understanding by calmly asking appropriate (non-inflammatory!) questions and listening to their responses, while also noting any subliminal messages portrayed by their body language. Then, to show you have genuinely listened to and understood them, say something to support this. You could say something like:

'I understand...recognise...appreciate...acknowledge...that's your view...opinion...concern...' (as relevant to the situation), then follow this with a 'linking' word or phrase, such as: *'however...'*, *'nevertheless...'*, *'in spite of that...'*, *'alternatively...'*, *'on the other hand...'*, *'even so...'*, and so on.

What is important, is to avoid the word *'but'*. *'But'* indicates not only that you are likely to disagree with them, but also that you may not have listened because you disagree! When we hear someone say a *'but'* in conversation, our first thought often is, *'I know there's a contradiction coming!'*, and then consequently switch off from listening. We are therefore more likely to hold the other person's attention by using a more effective linking word or phrase which indicates we are not automatically gong to contradict what they have just said, or disagree entirely with them.

105

STEP 2 – saying what you think

Step 2 is expressing what you think or feel in a calm, non-confrontational and assertive way. It enables you to directly state your thoughts or feelings without insistence or apology. You could say something like:

'My thoughts are....I feel that...I believe...I understand that...I am concerned that...my belief is...my opinion is...', followed by something relevant to what you are thinking or feeling about what they have said, such as *'there are other considerations...options... ways of dealing with this...'*

In extreme cases where you believe someone is being rude or offensive in some way, then you may consider saying calmly and directly that you find what they have said *'offensive'*, *'inconsiderate'*, *'rude'*, or *'patronising'*.

STEP 3 – expressing your level of agreement (or disagreement) and / or what you want or expect to happen

Step 3 is essential so that you can indicate in a clear and straightforward way the extent of your agreement (or disagreement) and/or action or outcome you want, without hesitancy or insistence. You could say something like:

'Therefore, I disagree with you on that one...What I would like to see is...What I would like to happen is...'

A key benefit of using this approach and the suggested behaviour sequence is that you are not being impolite or disrespectful to the other person. And even if you choose to tell them directly that you find what they say is offensive, if this is said to them in an honest, calm and non-emotive way, I would argue that you are not being rude and insulting them, but that you are genuinely expressing how you feel, which nobody could dispute.

Since behaviour breeds similar behaviour, assertive behaviour is more likely to trigger an assertive response from others and therefore lead to a better outcome. What is important is that assertiveness is established and respect is both shown and expected in a non-emotive and non-confrontational way. And if someone is being aggressively offensive and you remain calm and assertive, then it is more likely (but not guaranteed!) that they will make appropriate adjustments and start behaving in an assertive, rather than an aggressive way.

So if you tend to be submissive in difficult situations, then projecting yourself by practising assertive behaviour will improve your self-esteem. If, on the other hand, you are inclined to be aggressive in difficult situations, then toning yourself down by practising assertive behaviour is likely to lead to a more productive outcome.

Developing 'Team Engagement Rules'

> *'Coming together is a beginning. Keeping together is progress. Working together is success.'*
>
> Henry Ford
> (Late founder of the Ford Motor Company)

Introduction

Teams are formed and work together for a many different reasons. And depending on their role, people may be involved with a number of different teams, each with a distinct and diverse purpose. At work, at both strategic and operational management levels, people are likely to be members of a management team involved in specific project or business partnership teams. Roles and activities outside our working lives that also involve teamwork include not only the community groups and others we may be involved in, but the relationships we have and the way we interact with family and friends.

'Team Engagement Rules' (TERs) is a term for the behavioural ground rules defined and agreed by a team – rules to which each and every member of the team makes a commitment. TERs are based on the principles and values that are important to the team collectively, and act as behaviour guidelines in the way team business and interaction is conducted. The behaviours signed up to relate not only to conduct towards each other, but also to their shared approach to making and communicating team decisions.

To be effective, work teams need to have a clear vision, mission, values, and objectives for the organisation to which they belong. So if you want to achieve inspirational teamwork, ongoing team transformation and exceptional team performance, you need to ensure that:

- The team are clear about the vision they are striving to achieve and the values that underpin the way they work.

- Collective and individual time and effort is focused on clarifying and executing what is most important towards achieving the team's and the organisation's vision.

- The team's broad aims, and the specific objectives (with measurable outcomes) that support these aims, are clarified and agreed.

- Team culture inspires innovation through sharing ideas, and values contributions to these from others

- *'Constructive dissent'* is encouraged, along with giving and receiving constructive feedback.

- *'Win/Win'* in all negotiation situations is sought both within and outside the team.

And to underpin the achievement of these:

- 'Team Engagement Rules' (TERs) are agreed and established within your core team and as far as possible in wider working relationships.

TERs are likely to include emotionally intelligent behaviour such as: self-respect, respect for others, openness, honesty, self-awareness, an openness to learning and a willingness to change. But because values relate at a very personal level to character and what we stand for, it follows that it is no easy task to examine, clarify, articulate and agree the shared values a team believes in. The benefit of committing to abide by agreed TERs means, however, that there is a shared understanding of, and commitment to, the behaviour expectations, which helps the team to be both more efficient and effective in achieving its intent.

While there are likely to be a number of TER commitments common to every team, such as having clear objectives and providing mutual support, how these are formulated and presented will be personal and specific to each individual team. What is important is that all team members sign up to them and check that they are living up to the behaviours involved. The TERs should be regularly reviewed, their relevance re-evaluated, and appropriate changes made. A full review should be carried out whenever team formation changes or if there are any other significant changes in team circumstances.

The following representations vary in their style and approach, and are not designed to be exhaustive or prescriptive, but are merely examples of what may be included. The first example is taken from the TERs agreed between an operational team in the service industry, and the second example is extracted from the TERs agreed by a senior executive leadership team.

Operational service 'Team Engagement Rules'

Example of Team Engagement Rules as agreed by members of an operational service team:

- **Openness and honesty**
  - Encourage open expression of opinions.
  - Build and maintain trust.

- **Define and agree clear objectives**
  - Clarify and coordinate key service objectives.
  - Maintain enthusiasm and commitment to achievement.

- **Maintain focused discussions**
  - Stick to achievement of objectives.
  - Focus on work related problems.
  - Manage time effectively.

- **Maintain loyalty to the team**
  - Stand by team decisions.
  - Everyone to own the outcomes.
  - Support each other within the team.

- **Appreciate individuals' skills within the team**
  – Clarify and respect others' roles in the team.

- **Listen to and respect others' opinions**
  – Even if there isn't agreement!

- **Maintain a sense of humour**

- **Keep people informed**
  – Ensure everyone in the team is advised of changes and kept informed.

- **Ensure equal team involvement**
  – Ensure everyone has a say.

Executive leadership 'Team Engagement Rules'

Sample *'Team Engagement Rules'* extract – as agreed by members of a senior executive leadership team.

(The complete *'Team Engagement Rules'* agreed by this particular team included additional headings *'Communication'* and *'Feedback'*, along with sub headings and supporting behaviours)

Relationships

- **Perpetuate informal engagement**
  – Schedule monthly *'no agenda'* team meetings.

- **Value people**
  – Recognise and value others' capabilities and contributions.
  – Value own and others' time.

- **Listen to understand**
  – Be open to, acknowledge and value others' views.
  – Check understanding.

Performance

- **Maintain strategic focus**
  - Prioritise and focus on strategically important tasks and issues.
  - Reflect on the emotional impact of decisions as well as the business impact.
  - Take corporate responsibility for decisions, and demonstrate loyalty to them.
  - Apply best practice to the structure and process of meetings.

(Additional sub headings included under *'Performance'* were *'Take and manage risk'* and *'Maximise output/Exercise influence'*, along with their supporting behaviours.)

Development

- **Encourage personal development**
  - Maintain personal learning and development.

- **Sustain the teamworking ethos**
  - Invest in regular and continuing team development such as 'Away days'.
  - Commit to positive induction to team values for new members.

Effective Communication

> *'It's not what you say –*
> *it's the way that you say it.'*

Communication is generally understood to mean the imparting or exchange of information, ideas or feelings. And methods of communication include written, verbal, and any form of electronic communication such as telephone, fax and email – plus the all-important way we communicate with others through our body language and facial expressions. Listening is also important to effective communication, as previously covered in the *'Empathetic Listening'* section.

Effective communication is based on the four key elements of context, clarity, genuineness, and warmth – not forgetting the crucial need to ensure appropriate communication tone. Tone can be ascribed to pitch, volume or other subtle differences in the way we speak, or in the way we communicate to others through our body language, and can also relate to subtle implied messages in written or other forms of communication. In either case, tone can often be difficult to describe or articulate. (We may for instance say that we do not like the tone of someone's voice or the tone of a letter, but may also have difficulty in describing precisely *why*.)

Communication tones can be categorised according to the different behaviour types outlined in the *'Assertiveness'* section: aggressive (overtly or covertly), submissive or assertive. Effective and emotionally intelligent communication is firmly related to an assertive tone that is respectful of self, equally respectful of others, and open and honest in its meaning and expression. Examples of the kinds of tone likely to be perceived as aggressive (and also likely to cause offence) are: harsh, strong, strident, loud, vociferous, vehement, piercing, arrogant, disdainful, patronising and vulgar. Examples of the kinds of tone likely to be perceived as assertive are: calm, considerate, composed, thoughtful, reasonable, restrained, self-effacing, moderate and reflective.

In simple terms, and whatever method of communication is used, communicating effectively with emotional intelligence means:

- Clarifying the context of what you are conveying.
- Using clear, unambiguous and understandable words and language that is straightforward and clearly presented.
- Being genuine and honest in meaning and expression.
- Demonstrating the degree of warmth appropriate to the message and to the person or people to whom it's conveyed.

The following *'EQ Communication Engagement Rules'* may be useful as a checklist:

• Examine purpose
Examine the true purpose or objective of each communication – check what the intent is of the information you want to convey (what you want to accomplish from imparting it).

• Clarify ideas
Clarify your ideas before communicating them – analyse them internally, and plan how you want to communicate your ideas, before you start the communication.

• Consider the setting
Consider the setting when you communicate – by being aware of people, circumstances and environment, and determining what method, approach and tone would show consideration of these.

• Consult with others
Consult with others as appropriate – be aware of others' feelings, their need for information and any relevant procedures that you need to adhere to.

• Be conscious of body language
Be conscious of your body language – ensure you're giving out the appropriate message in your body language and tone of voice.

- **Use appropriate language**

Use appropriate language for the recipients – check that the words and expressions you convey are appropriate to the people concerned, ensuring you avoid the use of jargon or terminology irrelevant to them.

- **Convey something of value**

Use the opportunity to convey something of help or value – consider others' interests and needs, and use the opportunity to provide information that will be of value or help to them.

- **Match communication with action**

Ensure your actions support your communication – do what you say you will! (Or explain fully if you are genuinely unable to meet a promised commitment.)

- **Follow up**

Follow up on communication to check understanding – ask questions as required, and always use *relevant* questions.

- **Understand first**

Seek first to *understand*, then to be *understood* – and listen in order to understand not to respond!

- **Show respect**

Demonstrate equal respect for self and others – do this in all types of communication and in all circumstances.

- **Principles and values**

Ensure that all communication is aligned with your principles and values, and demonstrates your personal authenticity.

EQ Renewal Balance

EQ renewal balance is about maintaining and developing the spiritual, intellectual, physical and emotional dimensions that contribute to being emotionally intelligent and sustaining overall wellbeing. Balance is important to ensure that the interrelated and interdependent dimensions involved are in equilibrium, and investment is made at appropriate times and at the right level to maintain a *'steady state'*.

EQ Renewal Balance Model

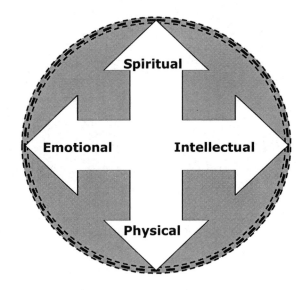

Spiritual renewal dimension

The spiritual renewal dimension means reflection on the purpose of what you are striving to achieve in both your personal and professional life and in your contribution to society. It requires investment in thinking time on the spiritual context of your life, the guiding principles and values that influence your conscience, your motives and priorities. It also means thinking, in a positive sense, about the legacy you want to leave and how you wish to be remembered.

Physical renewal dimension

The physical renewal dimension is about investment in general health and wellbeing. The obvious health benefits of regular physical exercise are well publicised as are the merits of a balanced diet and the need for rest and recuperation. But physical renewal is also about taking the time to appreciate the natural environment, by consciously observing, valuing and savouring the beauty of the world around us and allowing it to enhance a sense of wellbeing.

Intellectual renewal dimension

Intellectual renewal requires a commitment to learning and an interest and curiosity in people, the environment and life in general. Analytical thinking and reflection, stimulating reading and research, professional development, general education and training and development programmes all play a part. But it's also about building conscious awareness, exploiting learning potential from a wide range of experiences, and expanding your mind to encompass the benefit of learning and development in its widest sense.

Emotional renewal dimension

Emotional renewal is about conscious reflection on your own emotional wellbeing, while also being aware of how your behaviour impacts on others. It means developing and maintaining a heightened recognition of your emotions and reflecting on whether the experiences associated with these are beneficial or detrimental. There are obvious emotional payoffs in being able to do the things that inspire you and in spending time with the people you have positive relationships with. But if you find yourself spending too much time doing things that provide little or no inspiration, or with people whose company elicits only negative emotions, then it's time for a rethink and rebalance towards more positive experiences and more rewarding relationships.

Emotional Sagacity – the EQ Checklist

Emotional sagacity can be summed up in the three words confidence, clarity and courage: confidence in having better self-knowledge and understanding in your ability to learn and change; clarity in having principles and values to guide your behaviour; and courage in 'doing the right thing'. Above all, emotional sagacity involves discerning between the positive and negative influences on emotional wellbeing, making reflective and balanced judgements on how to deal with these, and developing and implementing appropriate action plans. Having emotional sagacity means:

Self-awareness, understanding and management

- Developing more conscious self-awareness and understanding through listening attentively to intuitive feelings, reflecting on your emotional responses to situations and whether they could be self-managed to more productive alternatives.

- Being tuned in to your body language and its impact on yourself and others, by recognising and understanding how your body's *'internal messaging system'* affects you, and how the body language you express is interpreted by others.

Self-development

- Regularly reviewing and evaluating your approach and behaviour and the emotional outcomes resulting from your decisions and actions – and being receptive to continual learning and change – i.e. being open to *'mind change'* rather than *'mindset'*.

- Being open and honest in evaluating your own strengths and weaknesses; actively seeking feedback about your behaviour and performance, noting this non-defensively and changing behaviour where needed, including acknowledging openly and honestly when in the wrong – and apologising sincerely.

Awareness and understanding of others

- Developing more conscious awareness of others' body language signals, the emotions they may be experiencing in the situation they're in, what their priorities might be – and an appropriate way to deal with these.

- Demonstrating empathy with and concern for others by showing a genuine interest in (and understanding of) their concerns, values, beliefs, likes, dislikes and priorities – and striving to build effective relationships with them.

Ethical guidance

- Showing personal integrity by having and expressing a clear framework of principles and values – having a *'moral compass'* to guide your behaviour.

- Maintaining principled beliefs, commitment and effort in spite of setbacks or opposition, resisting personal pressures which encourage non-ethical behaviour, and working towards the resolution of moral dilemmas.

Dealing with provocation

- Remaining calm in difficult or uncertain situations, acting in an assured and unhesitating manner when faced with a challenge and standing up for your legitimate rights in a way that does not violate the rights of others.

- Standing up for others' rights in a way that matches your principles and values, while acknowledging, understanding and dealing effectively with both your own and others' emotions.

- Distinguishing clearly between fact and opinion, making constructive efforts to resolve disagreements, and focusing on achieving solutions – especially when handling emotional situations.

Effective engagement

- Communicating to others in a clear, concise and genuine way that demonstrates an understanding of context, and conveying your message with an appropriate degree of warmth.

- Adopting communication styles appropriate to listeners and situations, selecting a relevant time and place and speaking clearly with a steady tone, standard pitch and even pace.

- Connecting with others and genuinely trying to understand them by listening attentively, and by being prepared to share your feelings and vulnerabilities.

- Valuing commitments and keeping promises, or explaining fully when unable to keep them and apologising as appropriate.

- Clarifying expectations, by clear and timely communication with others. This relates to both professional and personal communication – including communication of feedback expectations, clarification of differences of opinion, etc.

8

EQ Benefits

Emotional intelligence benefits both individuals and organisations. On a personal level, the benefits are both psychological and physiological; and on an organisational level, the advantages of an emotionally intelligent culture can mean not only a workforce with more productive working relationships, but gains in output and profits.

Personal benefits

The first and most important benefit of putting emotional intelligence into practice is that you are much more likely to be at ease with yourself, and to be positive and confident. In other words: to be *'comfortable in your own skin'*. Having a clear framework of principles and values through which you manage yourself and interact with others is the *'attitude foundation'* that provides this.

Having a better ability to engage emotionally with others also means you are likely to have more rewarding personal and business relationships – and more friends! In both your personal and professional life, engaging more effectively with people also means the potential to exert greater influence because relationships are more trusted and valued.

Becoming more aware of the impact of emotions on physiological state and the benefits of cultivating positive emotions to overall health and wellbeing are important EQ gains. And along with the physiological benefits, the psychological impact of developing more positive emotions is likely to lead to more motivation and improved work performance – or a perhaps a change of job as you seek a more rewarding and emotionally fulfilling role.

Organisational benefits

The increasingly fragmented, diverse and complex organisations of the 21st century require visionary leaders who commit to transformational change, and who provide inspirational focus, guidance and support to teams and individuals. A strategic *'big picture'* overview and high level EQ ability are the two key elements essential at executive leadership level. A worldwide poll of 900+ top executives recently conducted by Accenture discovered that what scares executives most (what they cited as their greatest challenge) was *'the ability to maintain a common corporate culture'*.

Development of an emotionally intelligent organisational culture of trust, openness, respect and cooperation between work teams, means that organisations can be more efficient and effective for a range of reasons. These include: more direct dialogue between people; fewer *'hidden agendas'* and a much more open and constructive atmosphere; issue resolution and problem-solving action agreement (before the problems become long-term obstacles that damage the organisation and the people); people with more confidence and competence in dealing effectively with difficult situations; the reduction of stress and time-wasting with destructive dialogue; and more innovation for product or service improvement because people's suggestions are respected, valued and listened to.

9

Closing Reflections – When EQ Really Matters

> *'The spectre of the future often overwhelms us to the exclusion of truly appreciating, and getting the most out of the day, the hour, the moment we are inhabiting.'*
>
> Eugene O'Kelly

Our feelings and emotions are the driving forces that underpin our attitude to life. And whether we acknowledge it or not, the profound importance of understanding and dealing effectively with both our own and others' emotions, impacts on all of us throughout our lives. And when we stop to reflect, it's generally not the tribulations of the day that profoundly affect us and prevent us from getting the most out of the moment, but the regrets of the past and the fear of the future.

While EQ matters at a level of interacting with people on a day to day basis at work, in society or in our social lives, when it really matters on a personal level is in building relationships with the people that mean the most to us. *'Please accept my apologies that come a lifetime too late,'* was the opening line of a telegram sent from her father to her mother, as told by Jung Chang in her moving portrayal of China's cultural revolution *Wild Swans*. The quotation offers a poignant reminder that living in the *'fast lane'* (by focusing on work or other achievements to the detriment of personal relationships) can often mean just that – time flashing by and all of a sudden a wondering of where the years have gone and whether time was invested in the things in life that are most important.

The payoff in being more emotionally intelligent towards our loved ones is a heightened recognition of the wider importance of emotional intelligence to relationships between humankind and the contribution we can make towards making the world a better place. I cannot think of a better way to conclude than by reciting an excerpt from *'This Life Mattered'* (author unknown):

What matters is not what we bought, but what we built;
not what we got, but what we gave.
What matters is not our success, but our significance.
What matters is not what we learnt but what we taught.
What matters is every act of integrity, compassion, courage
or sacrifice that enriched, empowered or encouraged others
to emulate our example.
What matters is not our competence, but our character.
What matters is not how many people we knew, but how
many people will feel a lasting loss when we are gone.
What matters is not our memories,
but the memories that live in those who loved us.
What matters is how long we will be remembered, by whom
and for what.
Living a life that matters doesn't happen by accident.
It's not a matter of circumstance, but a matter of choice.

Source reference:
http://www.poeticexpressions.co.uk/POEMS/This%20life%20mattered.htm

References

Reference has been included to a range of resources including websites, articles and publications as noted within the text. The following lists key texts and web-link information. Further EQ Learning Resources, including recommended books, articles, handouts, web-links and interactive resources can be found at www.eq4u.co.uk.

Apter International: www.apterinternational.com for information on motivational states and Reversal Theory.

Bartlett C and Ghoshal S., 1989, *Managing Across Borders: The Transnational Solution*, New York, Random House Business Books.

Bartlett C and Ghoshal S., 2000, *The Individualised Corporation*, Idahoe, Century Publishing Company.

Childs J. and Pardey D., 2005, *Mindchange – The Power of Emotionally Intelligent Leadership*, Cirencester, Management Books 2000.

Ekman P., 2003, *Emotions Revealed*, London, Orion Publishing Group.

Emotional intelligence meets Traditional Standards for an Intelligence: http://eqi.org/fulltxt1.htm#Emotional%20Intelligence%20Meets%20 Traditional%20Standards%20for%20an%20Intelligence.

Frankl V., 1997, *Man's Search for Meaning*, New York, Simon and Schuster.

Gladwell M., 2005, *Blink*, London, Penguin Books.

Hammond C., 2005, *Emotional Rollercoaster – A Journey Through the Science of Feelings*, London, Fourth Estate.

O'Kelly E., 2006, *Chasing Daylight*, Maidenhead, McGraw-Hill Education.

Salovey P. et al (editors), 2004, *Emotional Intelligence – Key Readings on the Mayer and Salovey Model*, New York, Dude Publishing.

Surcon International Inc www.surcon.com.

Watkins A (editor), 1977, *Mind-Body Medicine*, Edinburgh, Churchill Livingstone.

Wikipedia http://en.wikipedia.org/wiki/List_of_emotions (for a comprehensive list of emotions).

For a pdf of the References with weblink connections please email enquiries@mdplimited.co.uk, citing "EI90 references request".